Listowel Ontario in Colour Photos, Saving Our History One Photo at a Time

Photography
by Barbara Raué
2014

Series Name:
Cruising Ontario

Book 75: Listowel

Cover photo: 415 Inkerman Street West

Series Name: Cruising Ontario
Saving Our History One Photo at a Time

Book 33: Southampton
Book 34: Jarvis
Book 35: Hagersville
Book 36: Caledonia
Book 37: Simcoe
Book 38: Cambridge Part
1 – Galt Book 1
Book 39: Cambridge Part
1 – Galt Book 2
Book 40: Cambridge Part
2 – Preston
Book 41: Cambridge Part
3 – Hespeler
Book 42: Kitchener 1
Book 43: Kitchener 2
Book 46: Shelburne
Book 47: Alton, Mono
Book 48: London Colour
Book 49: St. Thomas
Book 50: Orangeville 1
Book 51: Orangeville 2
Book 52: Orangeville 3
Book 53: Dundas 1
Book 54: Dundas 2
Book 55: Dundas 3
Book 56: Stratford
Book 57: Hanover
Book 58: NewHamburg1
Book 59: NewHamburg2

Book 60: Waterdown
Book 61: Burlington
Book 62: Stoney Creek
Book 63: Seaforth
Book 64: Aberfoyle,
Morriston and Rockton
Book 65: Eden Mills
Book 66: Ancaster and
Mount Hope
Book 67: Jarvis,Pt.Dover
Book 68: Fergus
Book 69: Elora
Book 70: Elmira Book 1
Book 71: Elmira 2 & Area
Book72:St.Jacobs, St.Clements,
Heidelberg,Crosshill,Bamberg
Book 73: Linwood, Macton
Book 74: Wellesley
Book 75: Listowel

Other Books by Barbara Raue

Coins of Gold

Arrows, Indians and Love

The Life and Times of Barbara
Volume 1: Inventions That Have Enhanced My Life
Volume 2: Entertainment That I Have Enjoyed
Volume 3: East Coast Trips
Volume 4: Olympics Have Always Intrigued Me
Volume 5: Wonders of the World
Volume 6: Caribbean Cruises We Have Enjoyed
Volume 7: Animals
Volume 8: Storms and Other Major Disasters in My Lifetime
Volume 9: Wars, Terrorist Attacks and Major Disasters

The Cromwell Family Book

Laura Secord Discovered

Visit Barbara's website to view all of her books
http://barbararaue.ca

Listowel

Listowel is located in the municipality of North Perth, northwest of Kitchener/Waterloo, and west of Elmira on Highway 86.

Settler John Binning arrived in 1857 and was the first to create a permanent residence in the area. The community was originally named Mapleton, but the name was changed when a post office was established. The new name was chosen by a government official and refers to Listowel, Ireland (a market town in County Kerry situated on the River Feale, 28 kilometres, or 17 miles, from the county town, Tralee.) The majority of early settlers were of Protestant Irish origin.

In 1907, hydroelectric and telephone services came to the town with the Princess cinema. During World War II the theatre was renamed the Capitol and remains Canada's oldest operating cinema.

In 1871 the Wellington, Grey and Bruce Railway extended its line to Listowel. It was joined in 1873 by a second railway, the Stratford and Huron Railway, and Listowel became an important shipping point. The population doubled when industries, including a woolen mill, a sawmill, a planing mill and a tannery, were established. In 1891 the Morris, Field, Rogers Company Ltd began to manufacture Morris pianos in Listowel.

The Campbell Soup Company was a major local employer for 48 years, operating a frozen, foodservice and specialty food plant in Listowel. The factory closed in April 2008. The surrounding area is mostly agricultural land located on the Perth Plain, dominated by the beef and pork industries.

Table of Contents

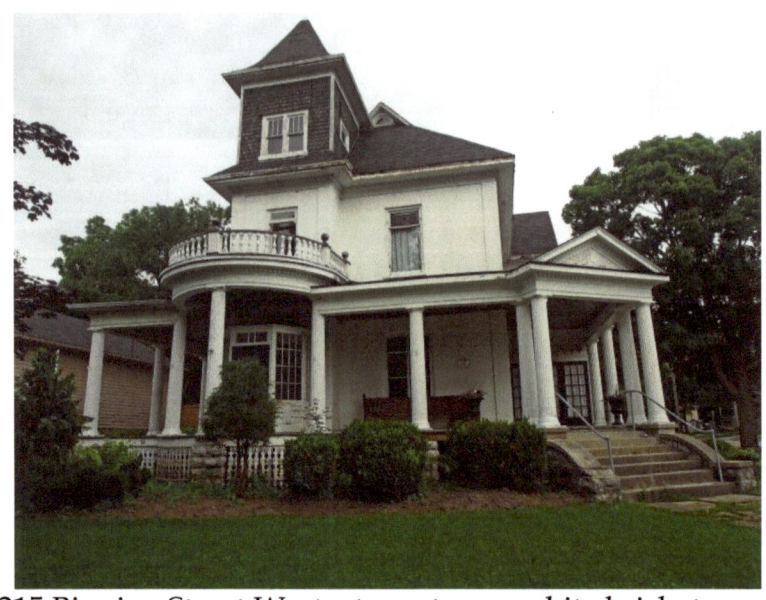

215 Binning Street West – two-storey, white brick, tower, dormer – originally this was a full three storeys high with a Mansard roof; a fire in 1922 damaged the upper level and a new roof was added in the Queen Anne style; spindle railing around circular balcony, Doric pillars, pediment

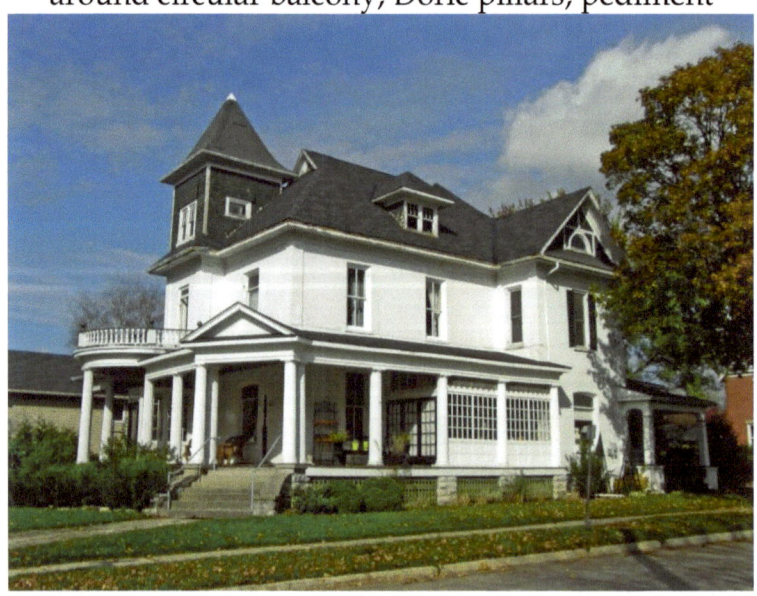

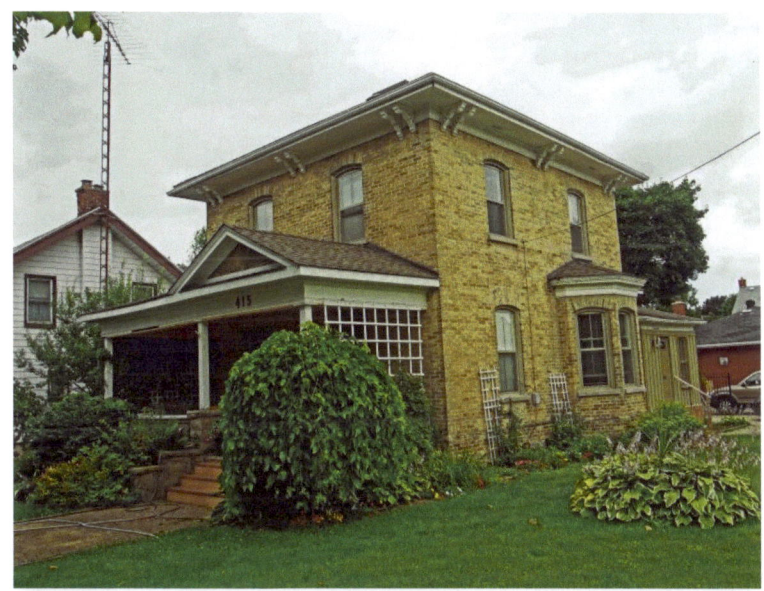

415 Binning Street West – Italianate style, cornice brackets, round bay window on side, pediment above verandah

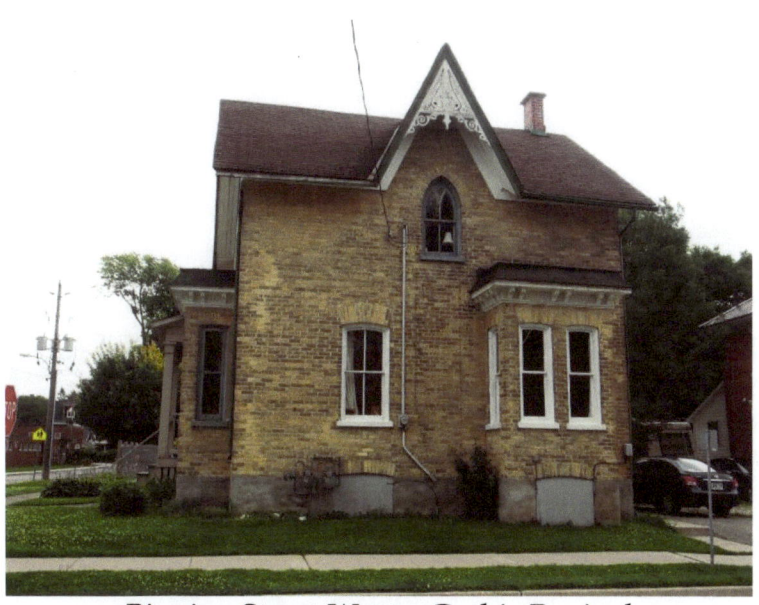

Binning Street West – Gothic Revival
Vergeboard trim on gable with finial, square bay windows

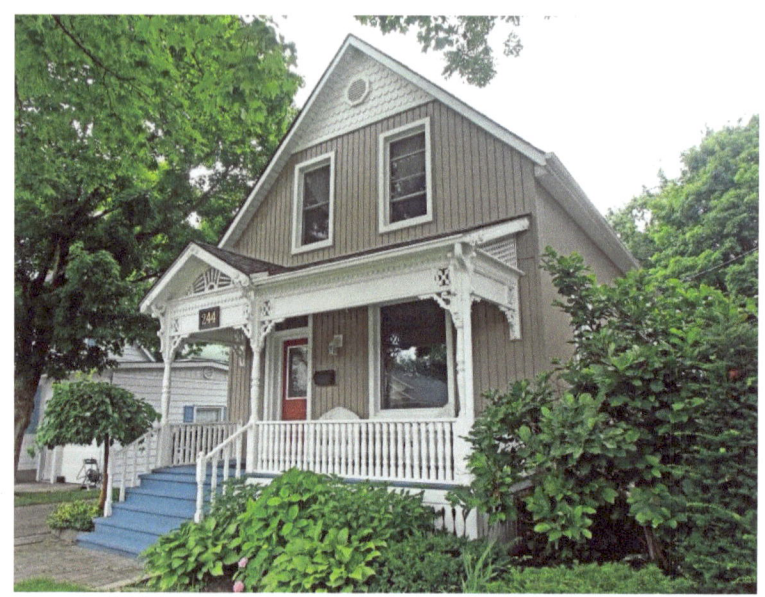

244 Binning Street West – Gothic Revival

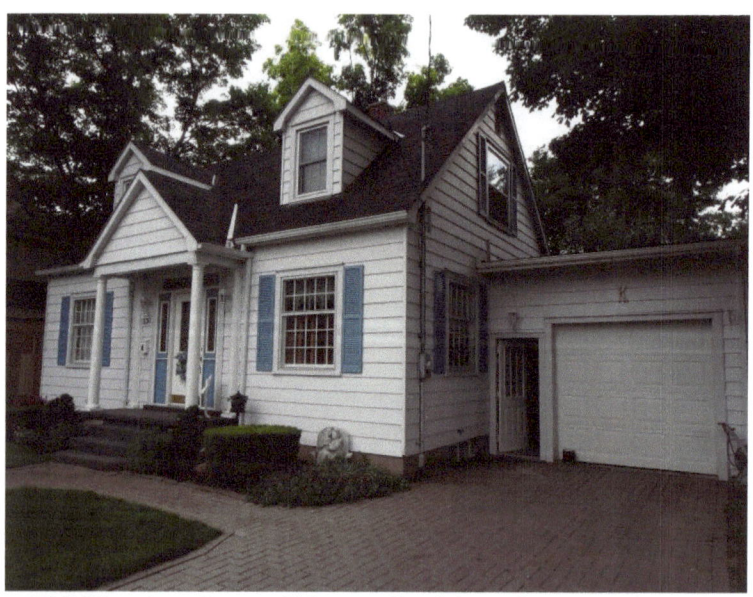

230 Binning Street West – Gothic – dormers in attic

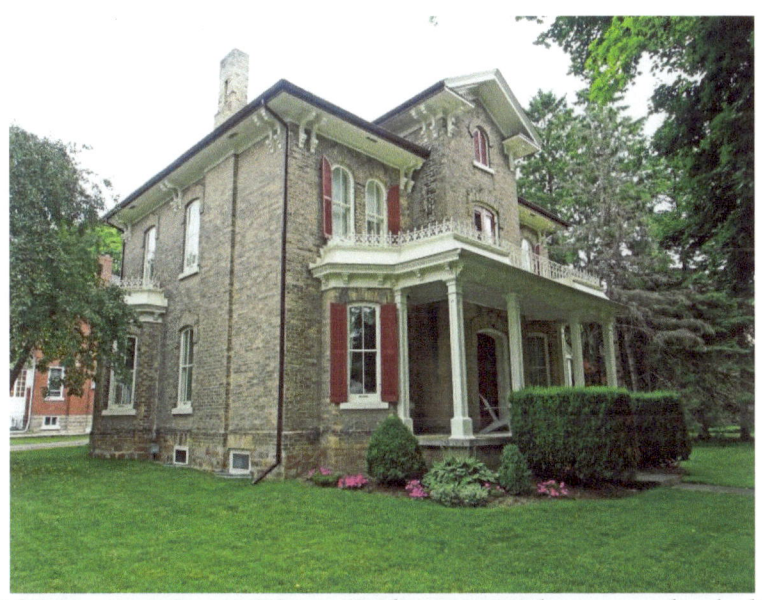

185 Binning Street West – Italianate with two-and-a-half storey tower-like bay, paired cornice brackets, balcony on second floor, cornice return on gable, built in 1872

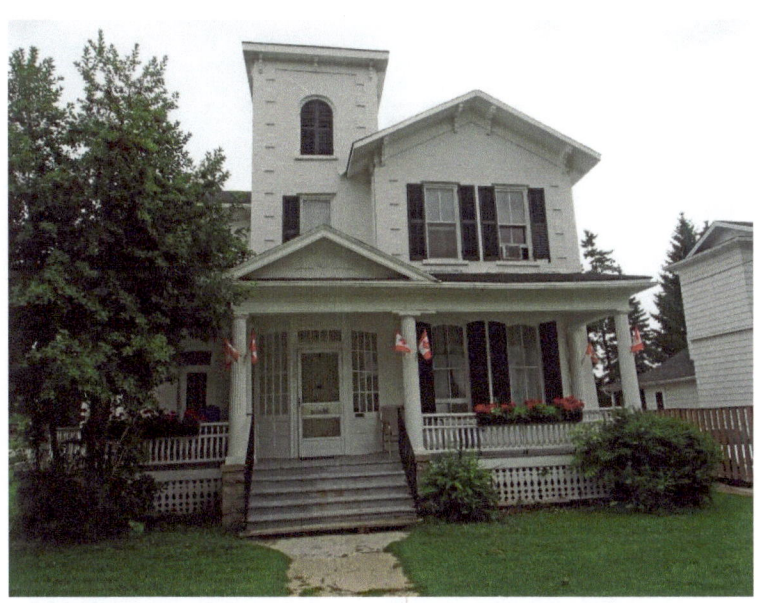

333 Binning Street West – Queen Anne style, tower, cornice brackets, pediment above verandah

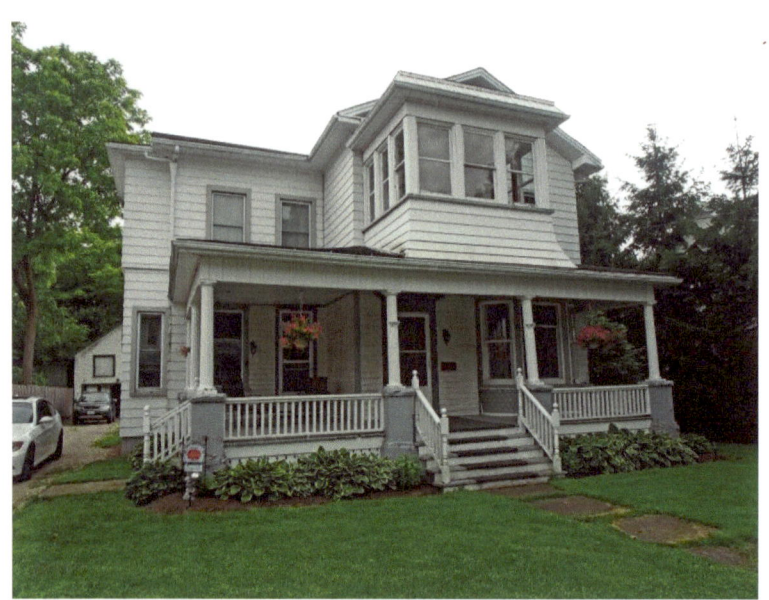

376 Binning Street West – Gothic with added enclosed sun porch above verandah

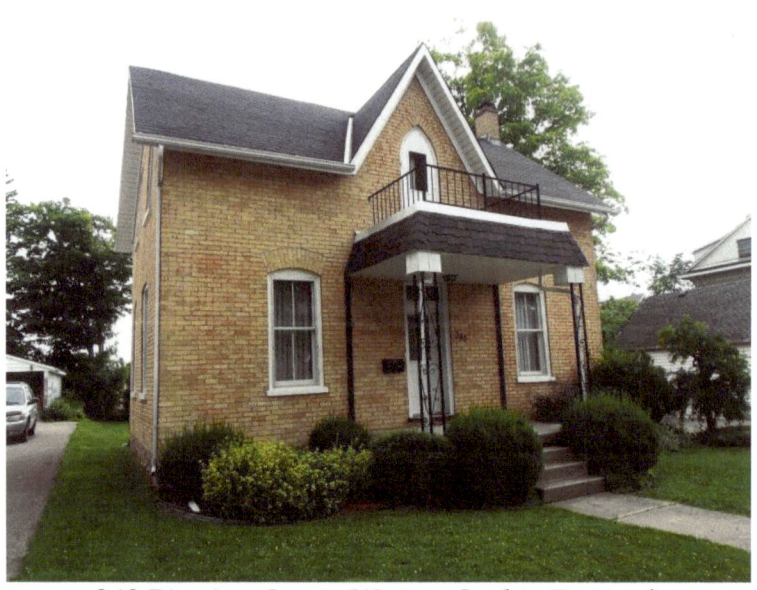

340 Binning Street West – Gothic Revival, balcony on second floor

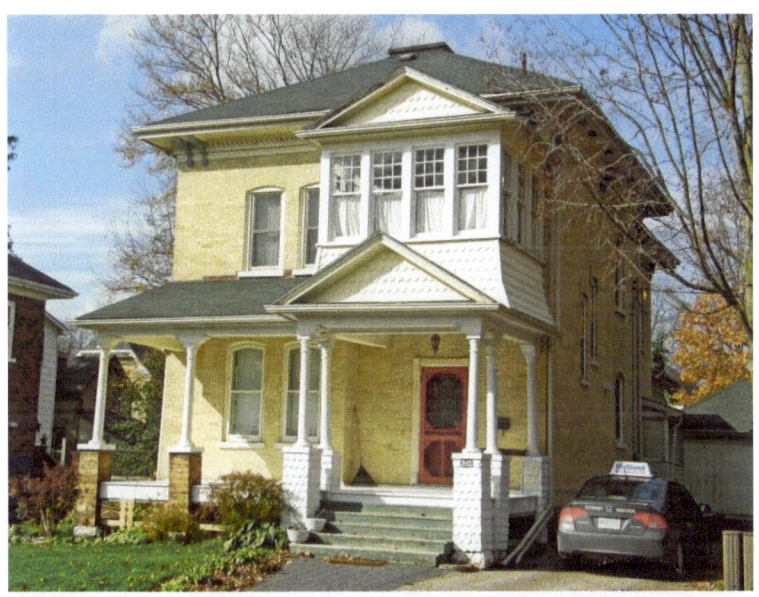

345 Binning Street West – Italianate, cornice brackets, pediments above verandah and above second floor with fish scale pattern in tympanum

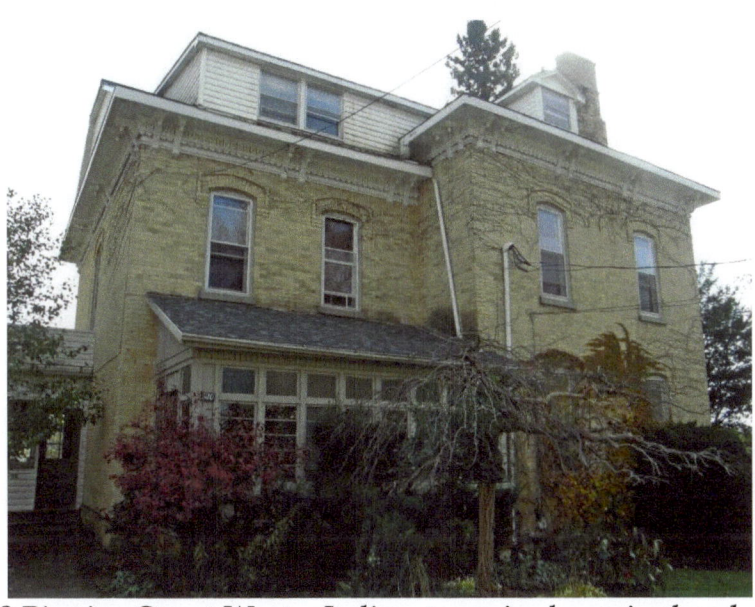

320 Binning Street West – Italianate, paired cornice brackets, arched window voussoirs, decorative cornice, dormers

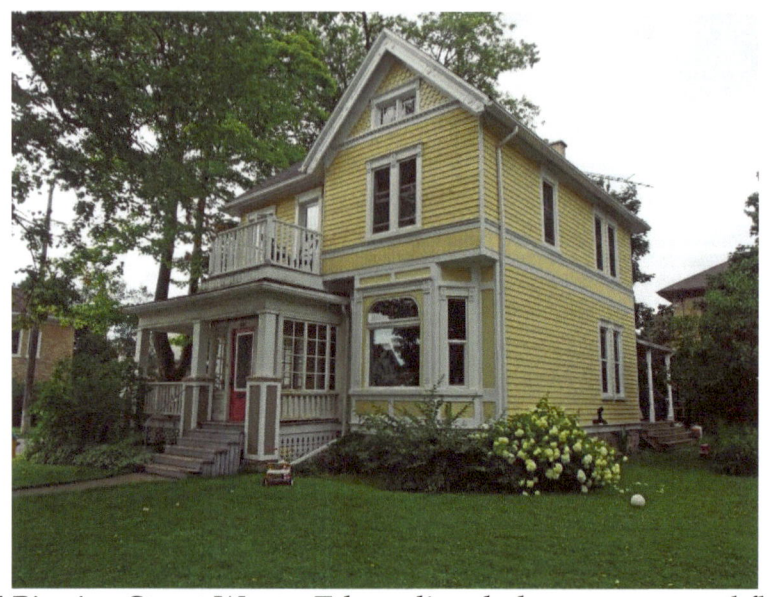

305 Binning Street West – Edwardian, balcony on second floor
Fish scale pattern in gable

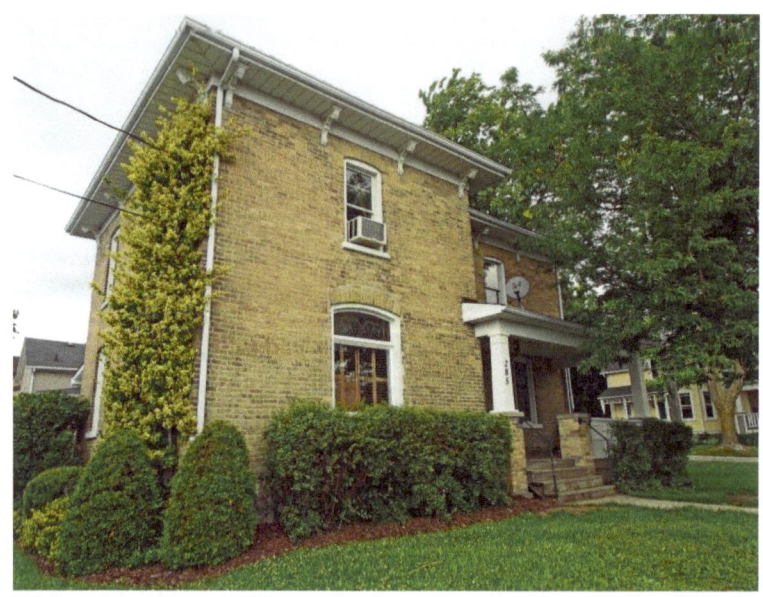

285 Binning Street West – Italianate, single cornice brackets

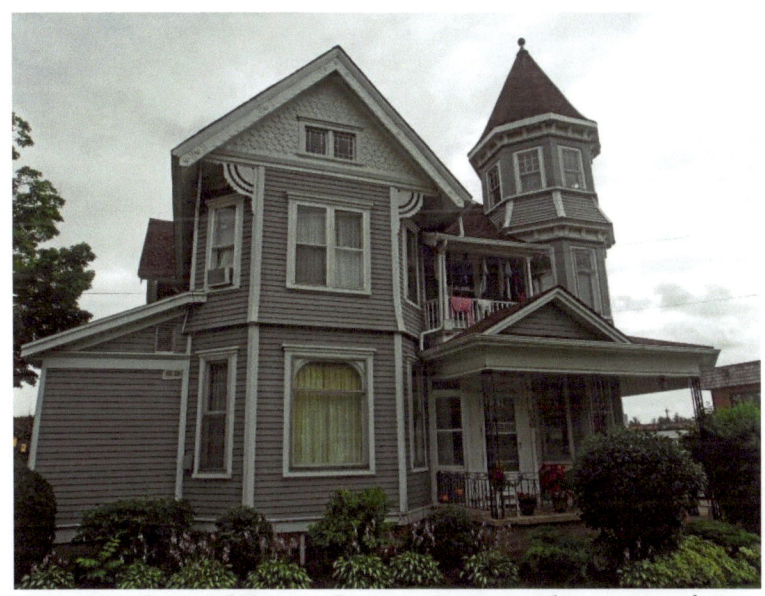

280 Binning Street West – Queen Anne style, tower, fretwork

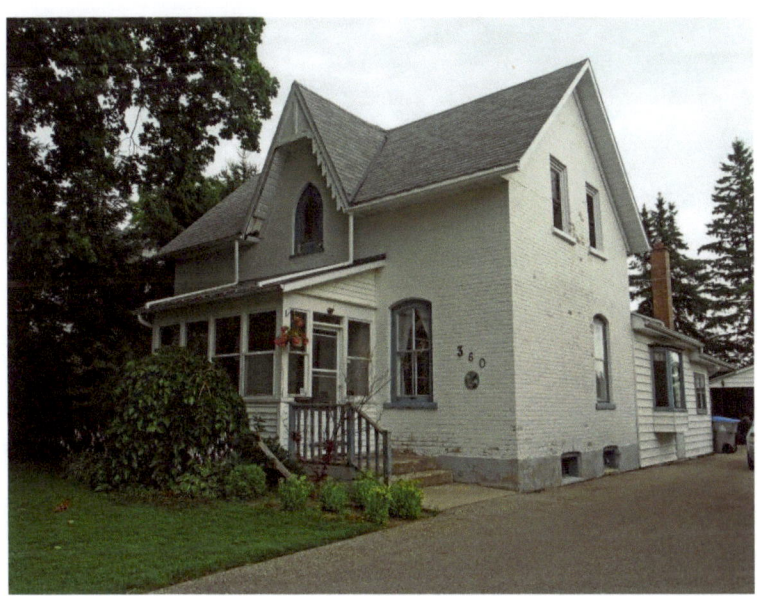

360 Binning Street West – Gothic Revival, Vergeboard trim

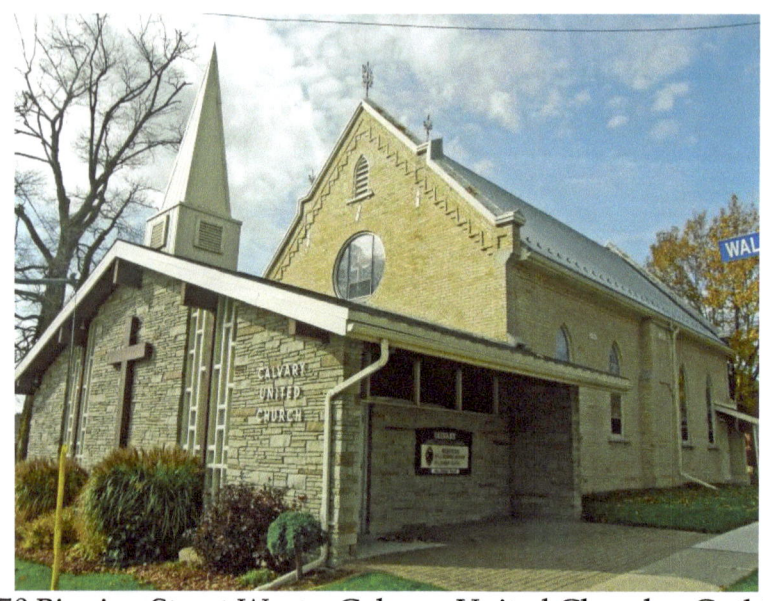

150 Binning Street West – Calvary United Church – Gothic, patterned brickwork on gable end, lancet windows

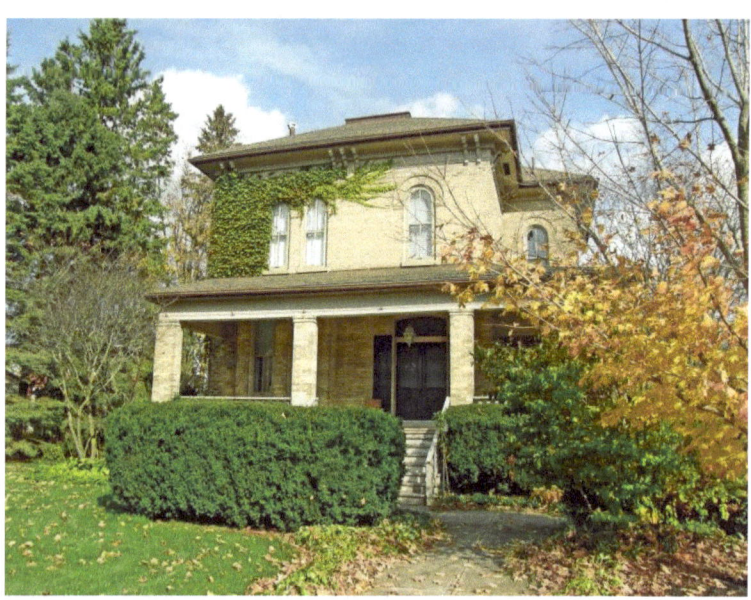

145 Binning Street West – built in 1880s – Italianate, cornice brackets, arched window voussoirs

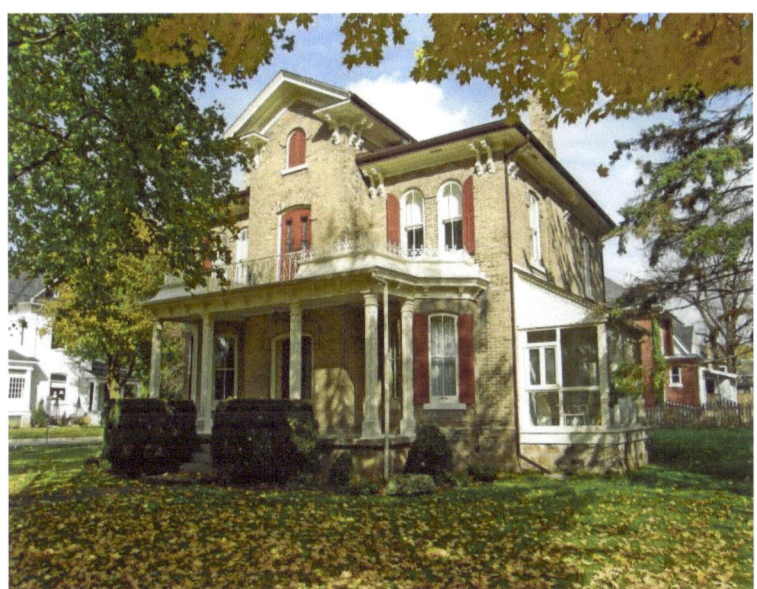

Binning Street West - Italianate, paired cornice brackets, two-and-a-half storey tower-like bay with cornice return on gable, balcony on second floor, iron cresting

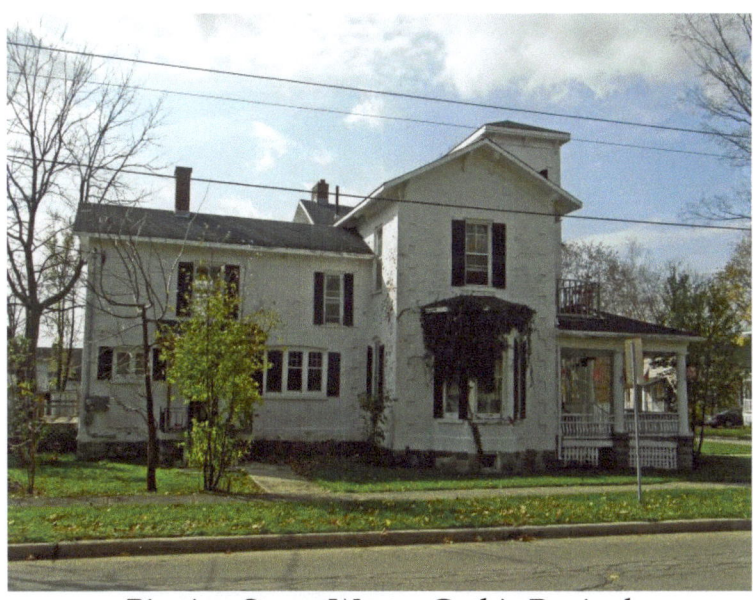

Binning Street West – Gothic Revival

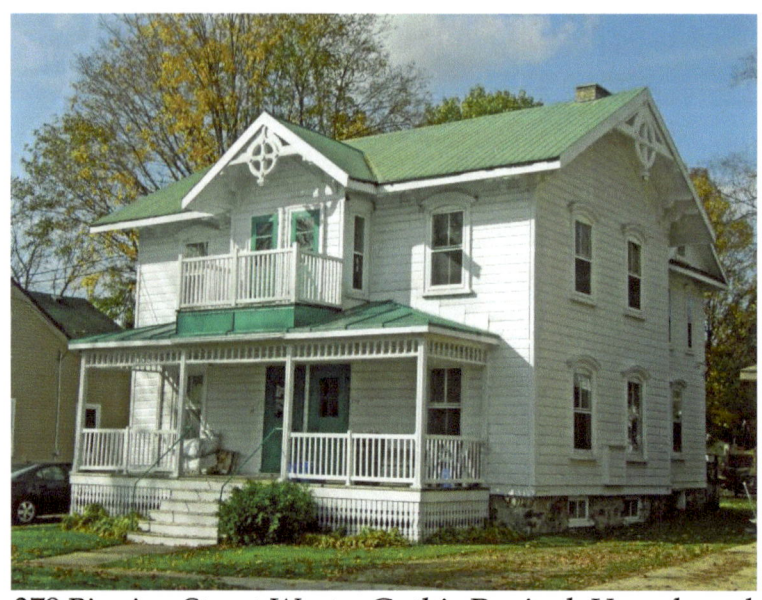

379 Binning Street West – Gothic Revival, Vergeboard decoration on gables, balcony on second floor

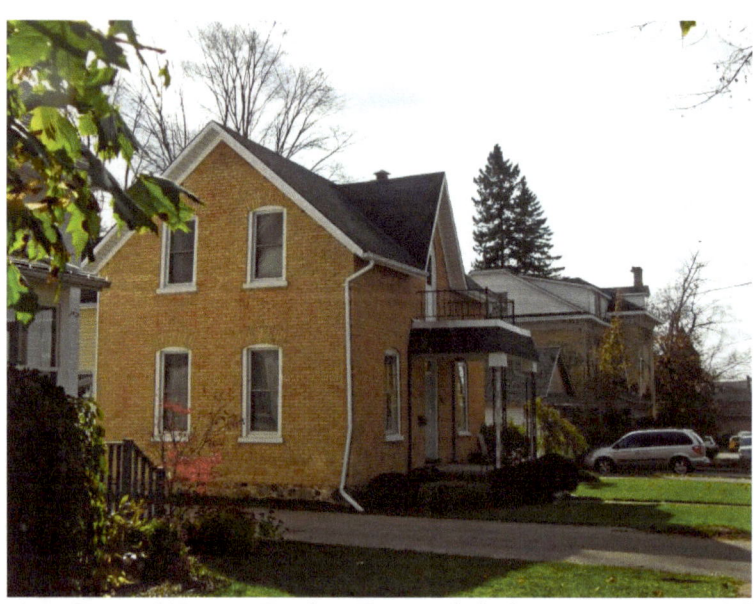

Binning Street West – Gothic Revival, balcony on second floor

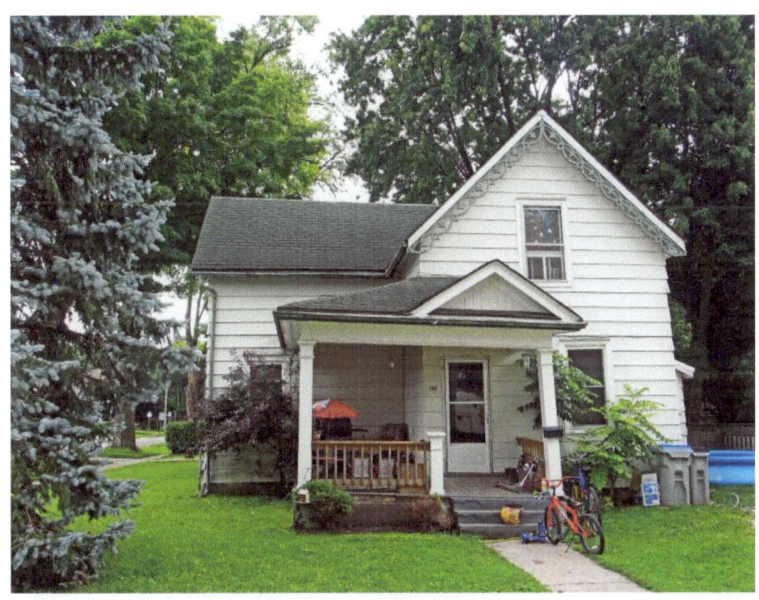

390 Livingstone Avenue North – Gothic Revival, Vergeboard
trim on gables, pediment above front porch

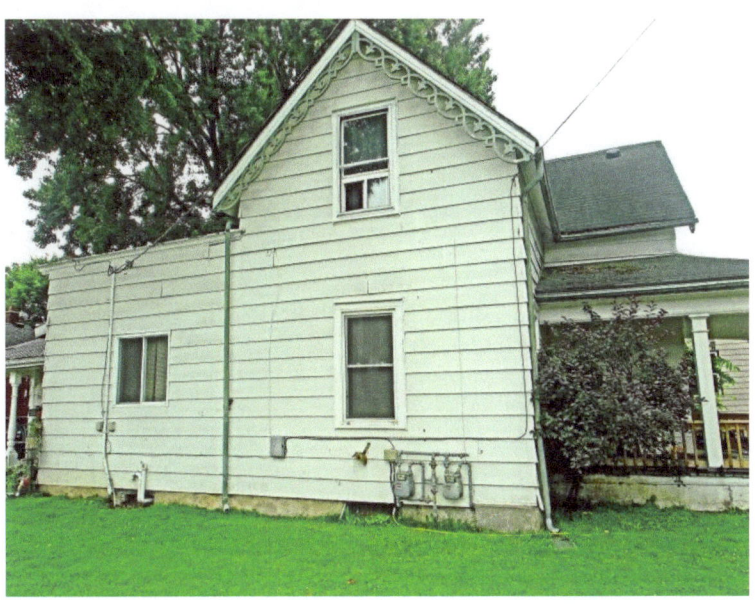

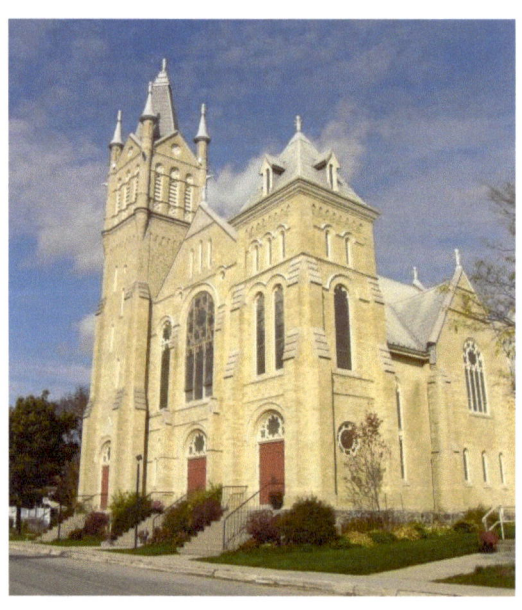

220 Livingstone Avenue North – Knox Presbyterian Church
Built between 1883 and 1887 in the Romanesque style with
lofty towers and turrets reflecting a strong Scottish influence

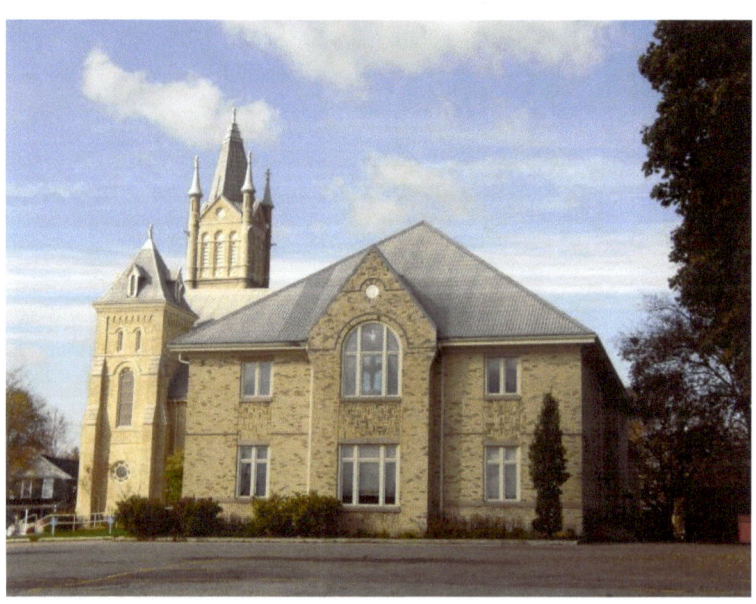

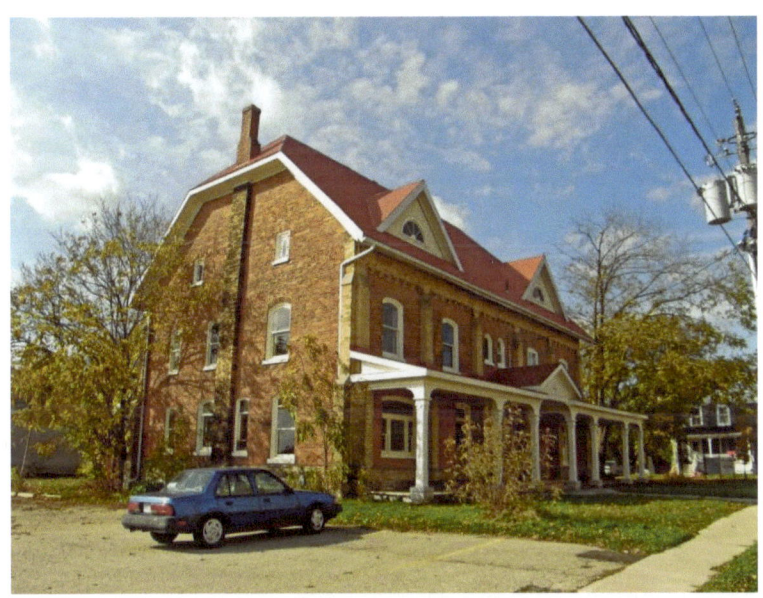

Livingstone Avenue North

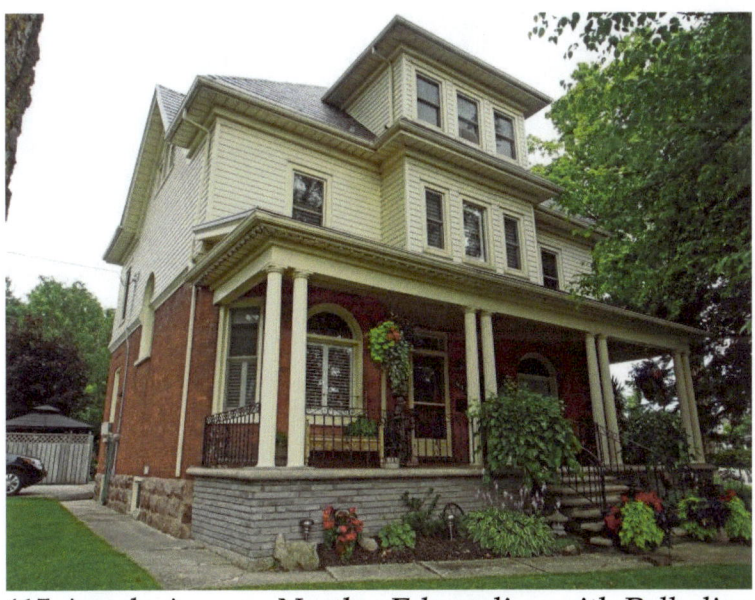

415 Argyle Avenue North – Edwardian with Palladian
window below side gable, dormer in attic, Romanesque style
round window arches on first floor, Doric columns

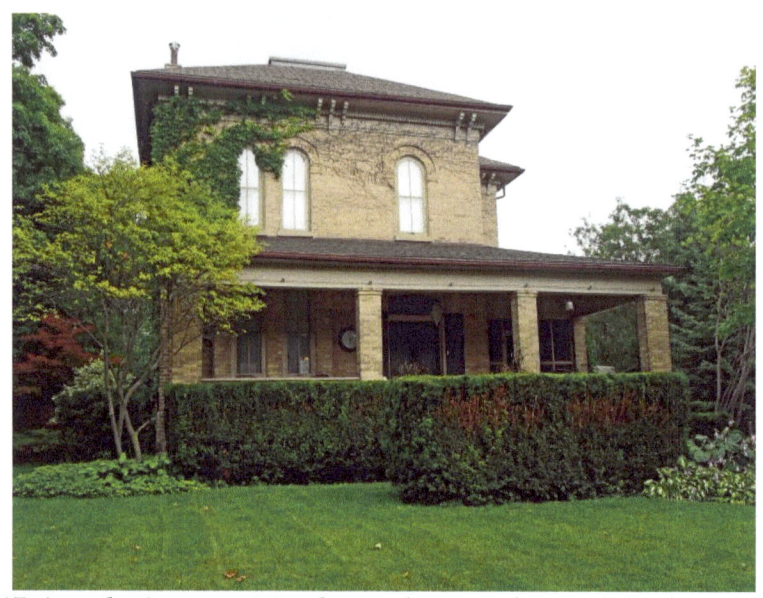

145 Argyle Avenue North – Italianate, hipped roof, cornice brackets, round arched window voussoirs

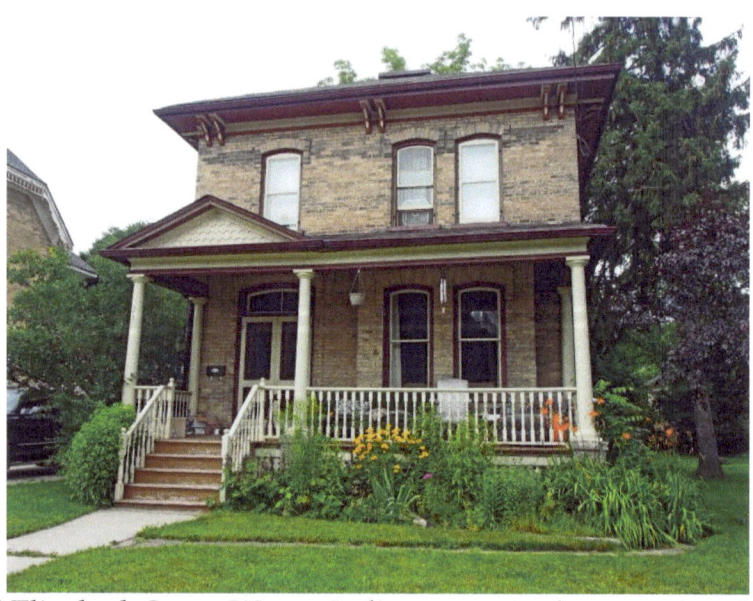

235 Elizabeth Street West – Italianate, paired cornice brackets, pediment above verandah, Doric columns

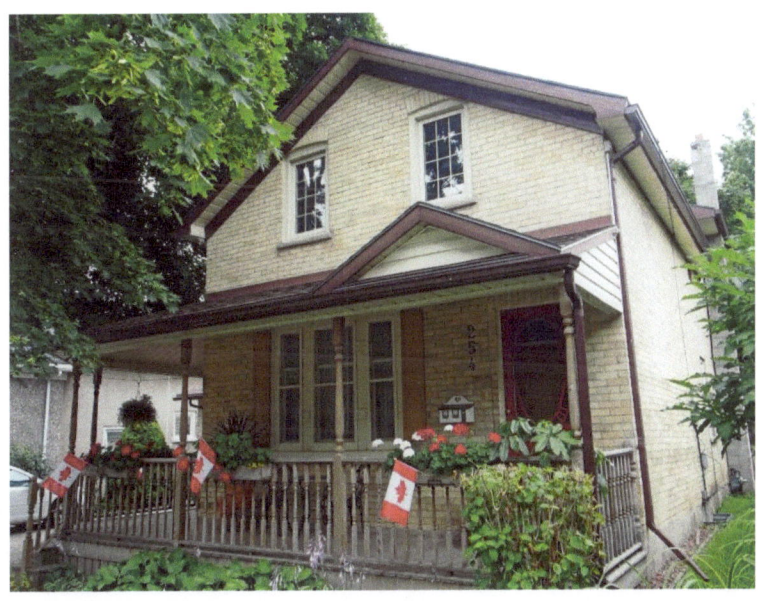

254 Elizabeth Street West – Gothic Revival, pediment above verandah

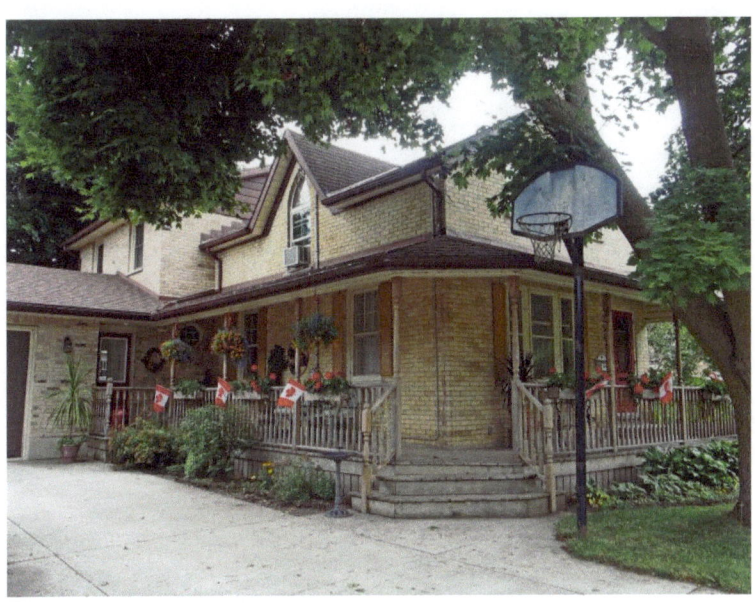

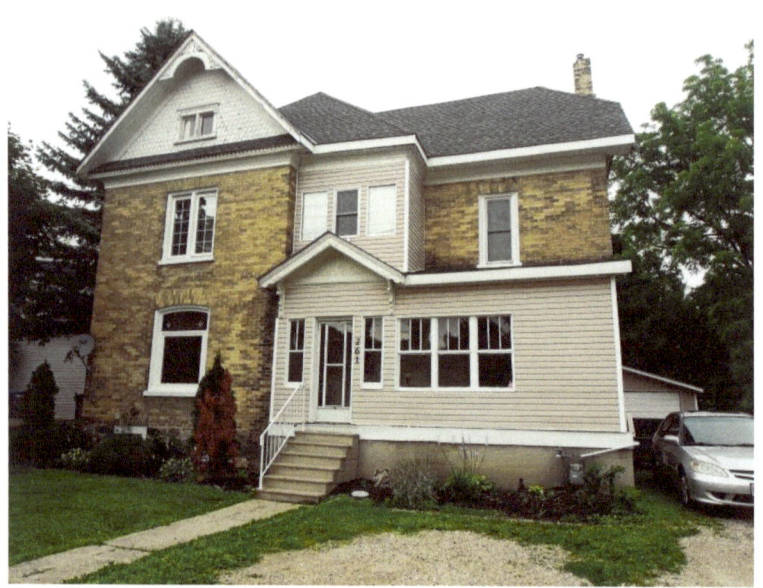
261 Elizabeth Street West - Edwardian

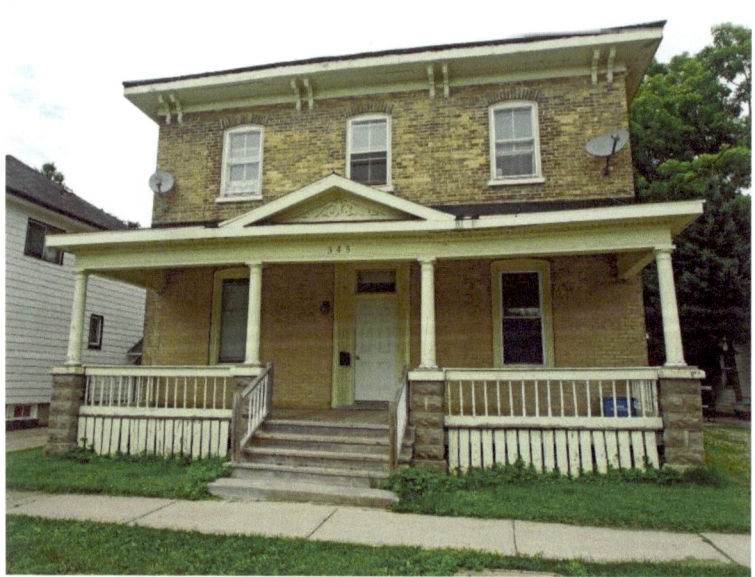
345 Elizabeth Street West – Italianate, paired cornice brackets, pediment above porch with decorated tympanum

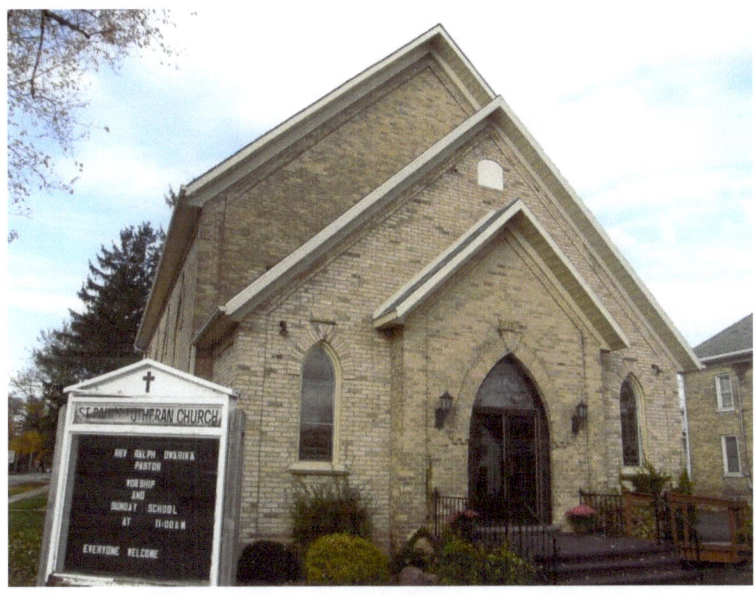

505 Wallace Avenue North – St. Paul's Lutheran Church - 1868

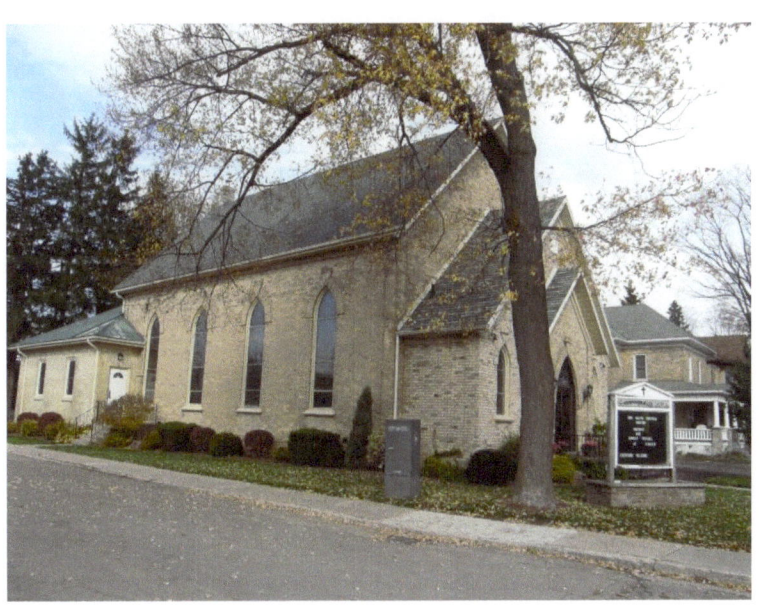

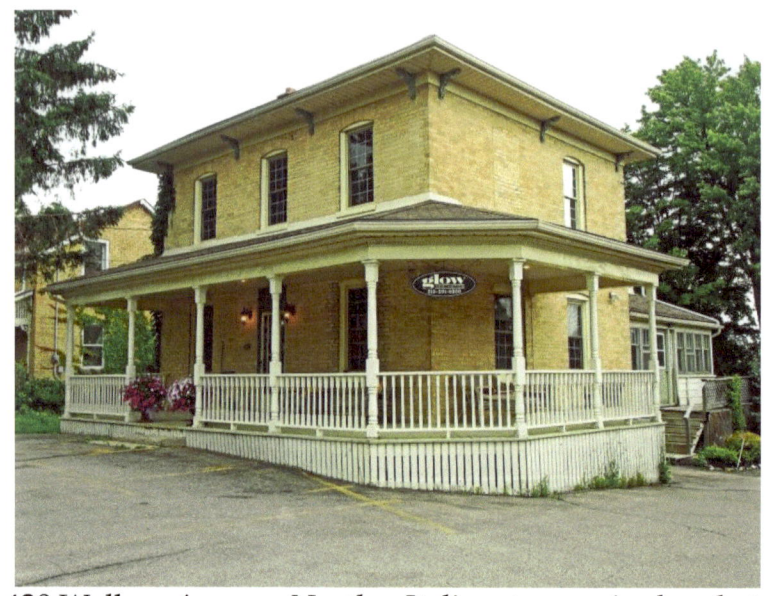

420 Wallace Avenue North – Italianate, cornice brackets

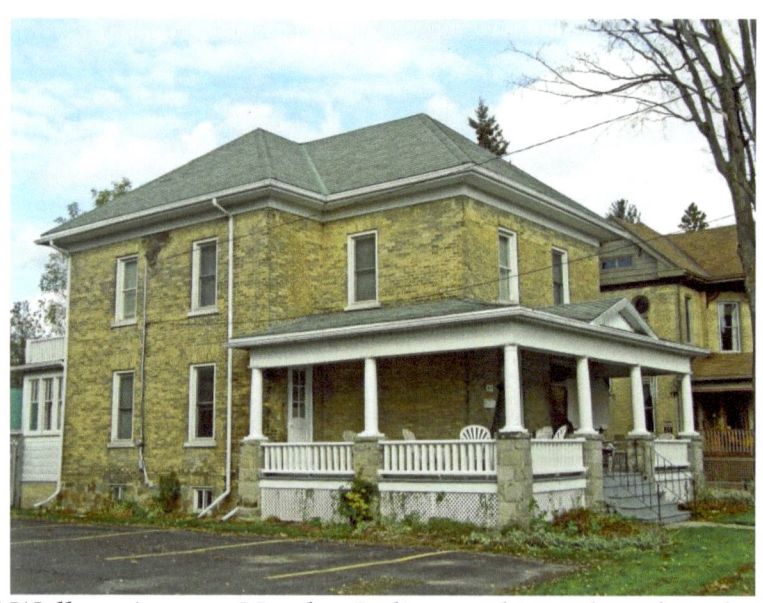

525 Wallace Avenue North – Italianate, hipped roof, pediment

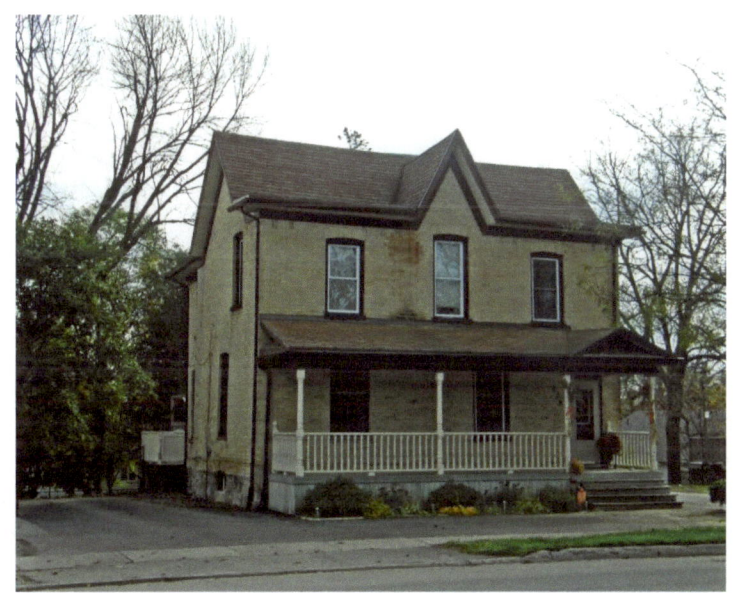

478 Wallace Avenue North – Gothic Revival

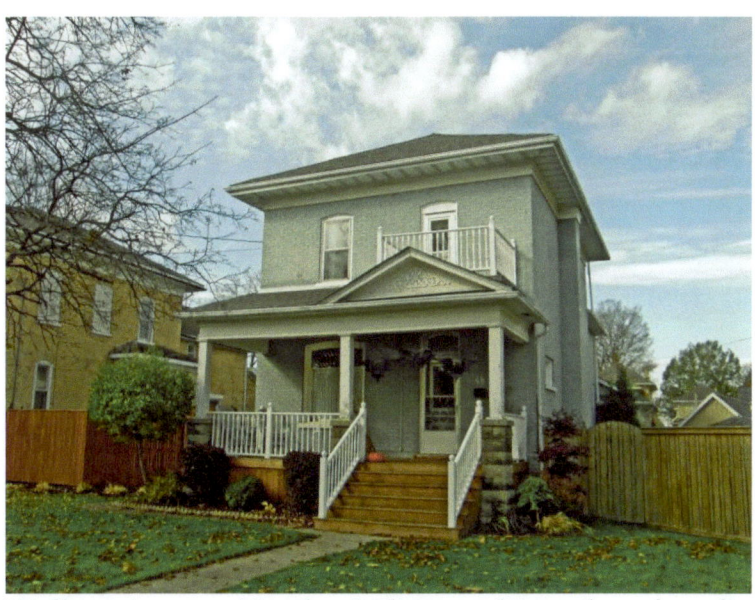

485 Wallace Avenue North – Italianate, hipped roof, pediment

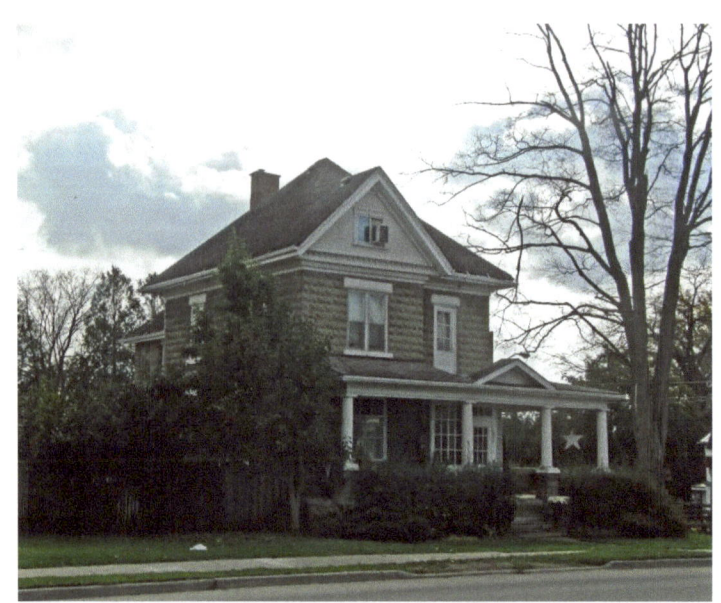

454 Wallace Avenue North

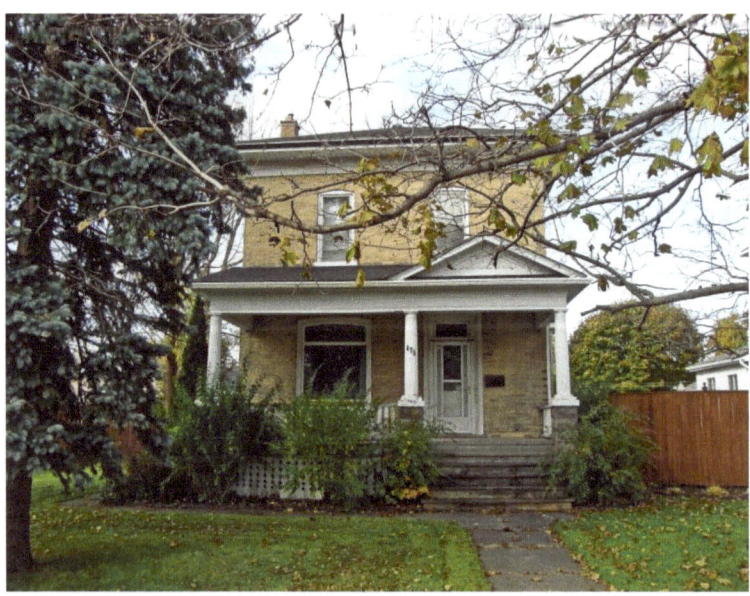

475 Wallace Avenue North – Italianate, pediment

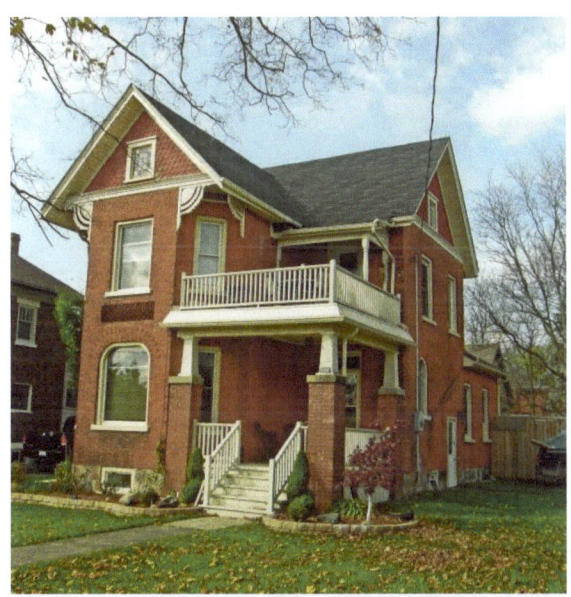

445 Wallace Avenue North – Edwardian, fretwork,
second floor balcony

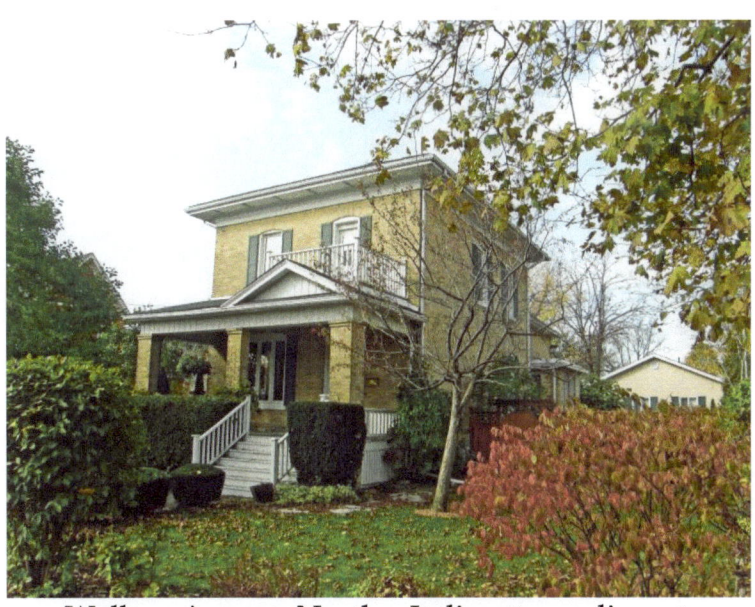

Wallace Avenue North – Italianate, pediment,
second floor balcony

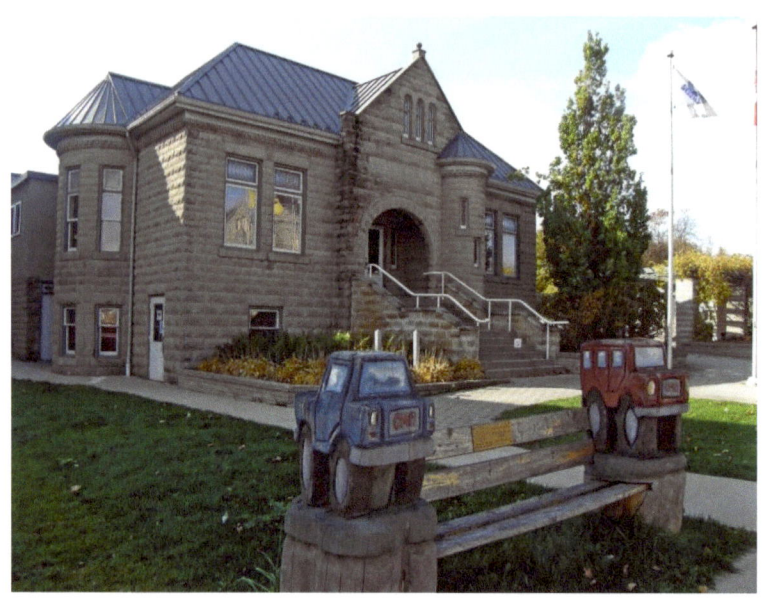

330 Wallace Avenue North – North Perth Public Library
Built in 1907

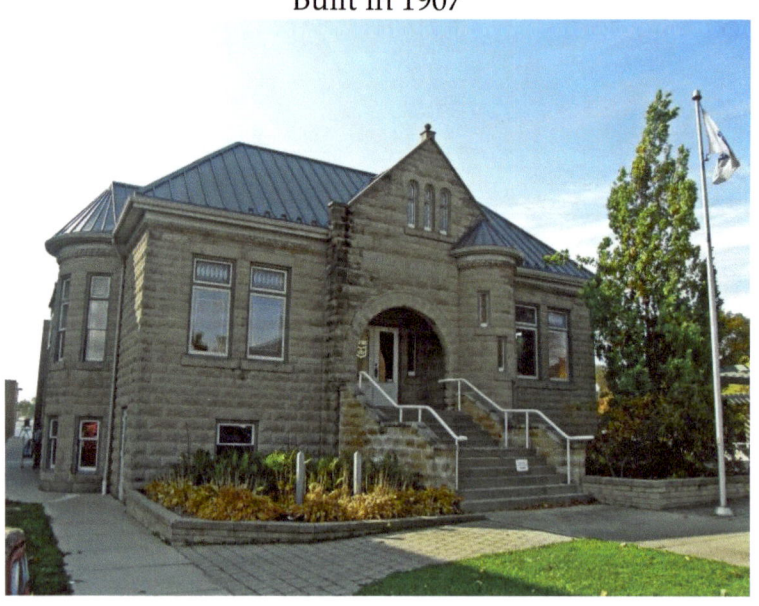

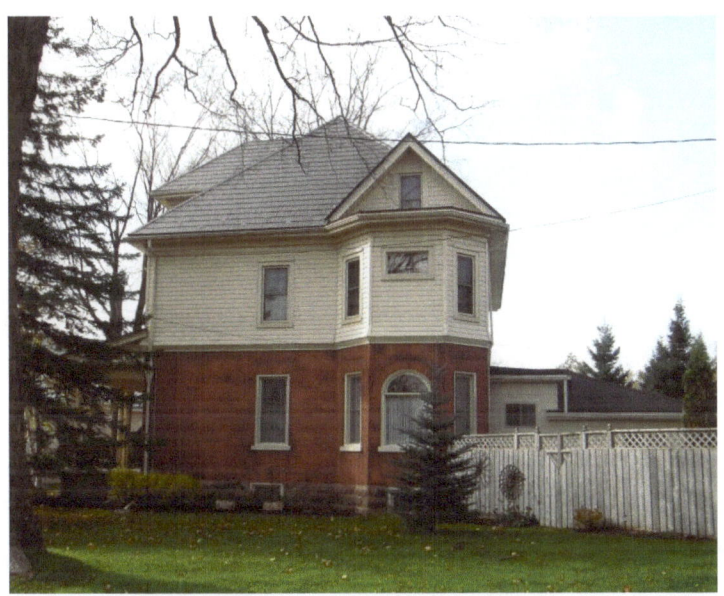

Wallace Avenue North

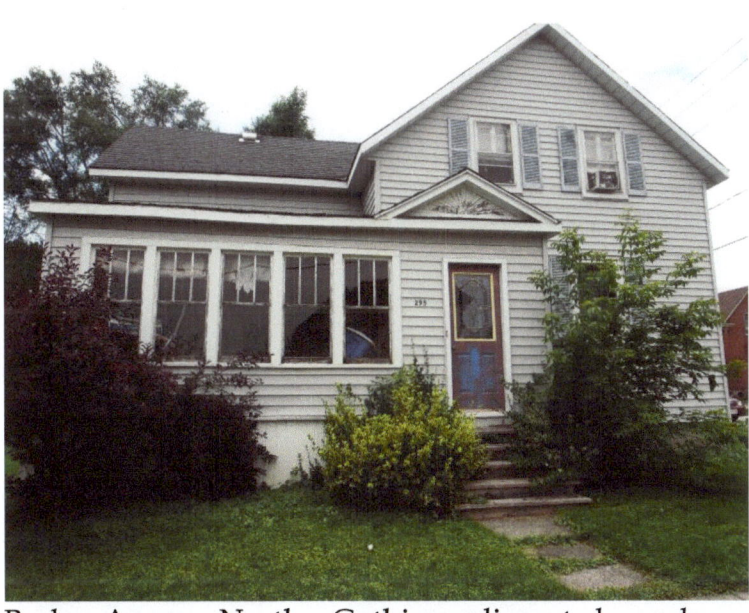

295 Barber Avenue North – Gothic, pediment above door with
decorated tympanum

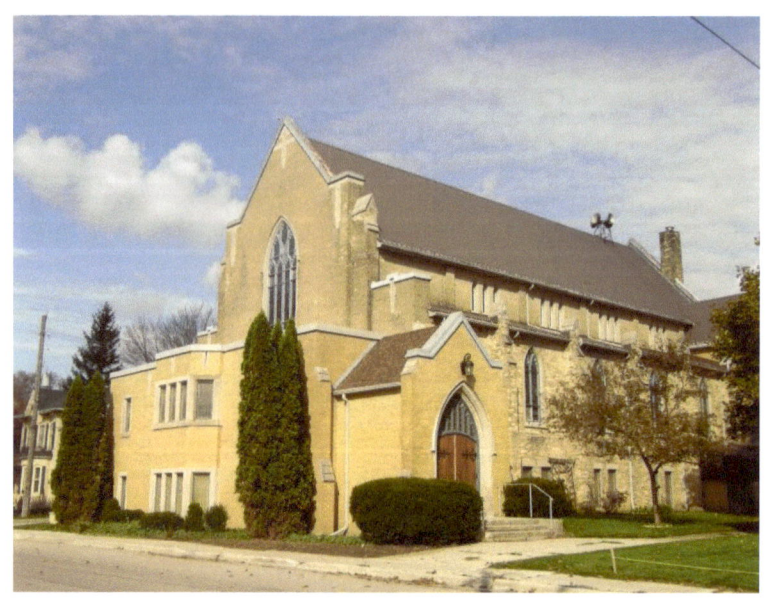

230 Barber Avenue North – Trinity United Church - Gothic

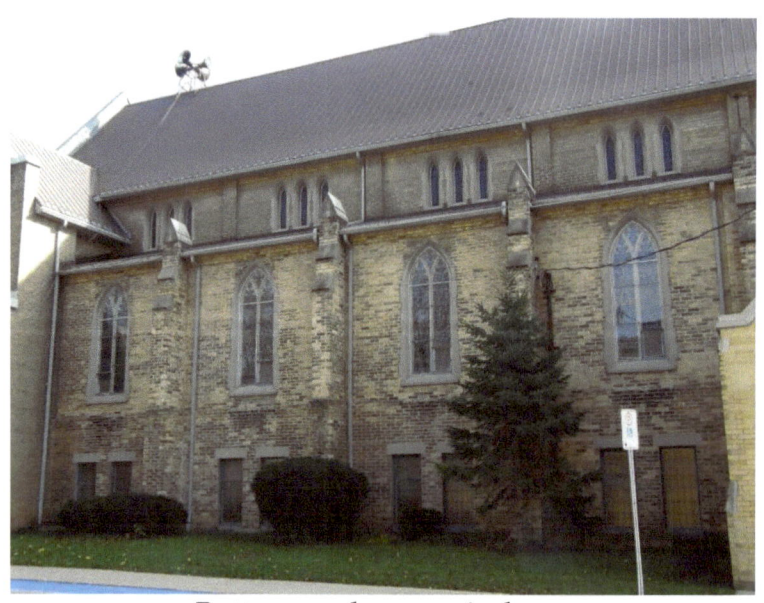

Buttresses, lancet windows

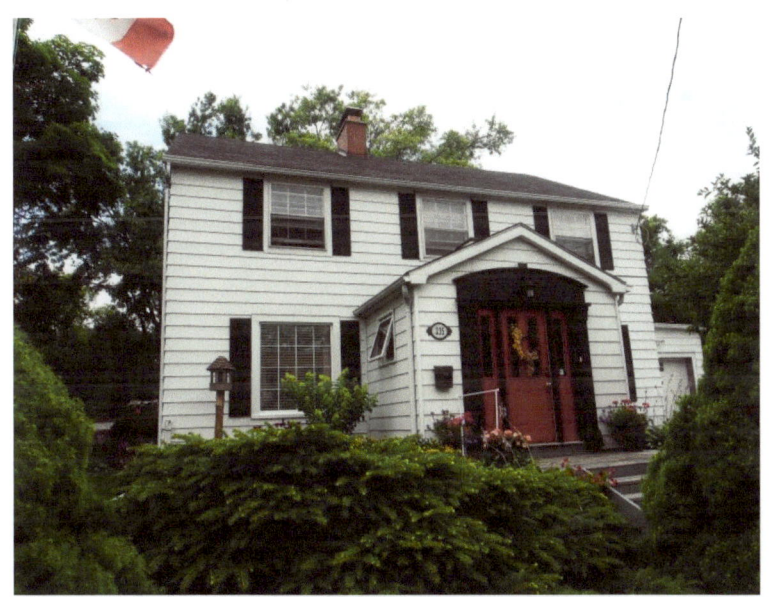

235 Barber Avenue North

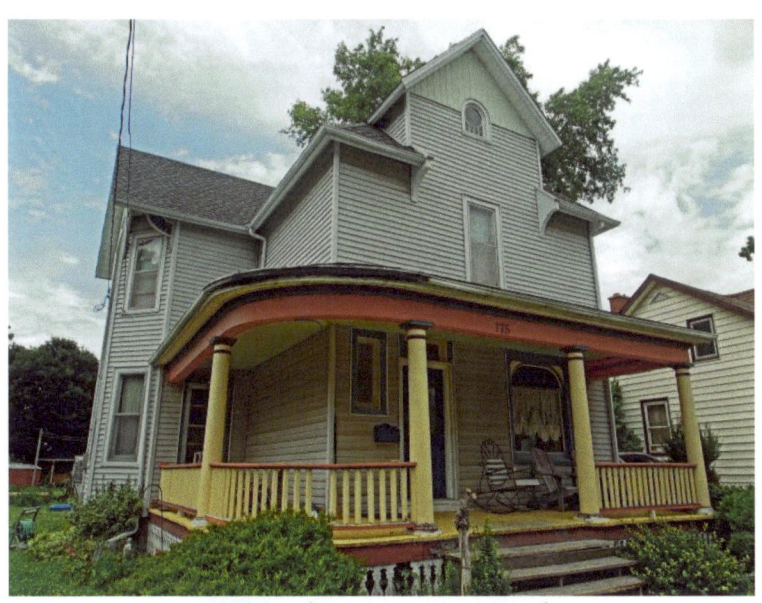

175 Barber Avenue North

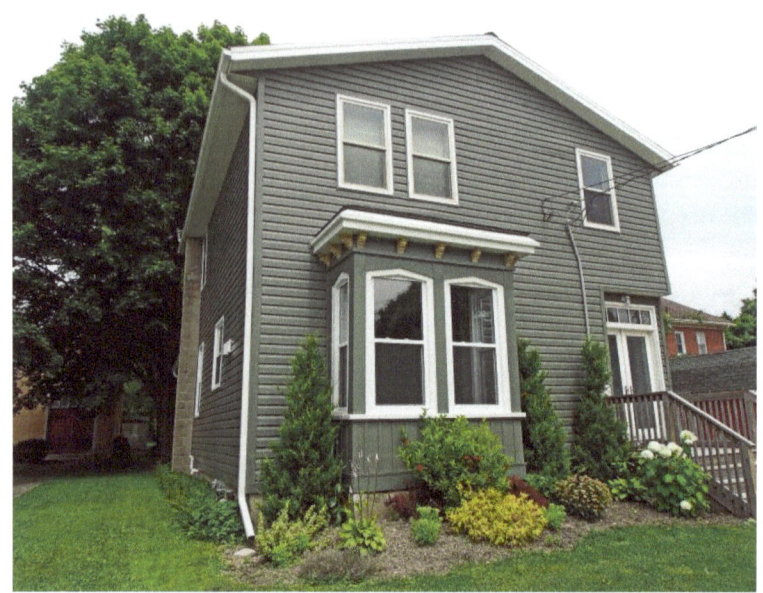

245 Inkerman Street West – Gothic

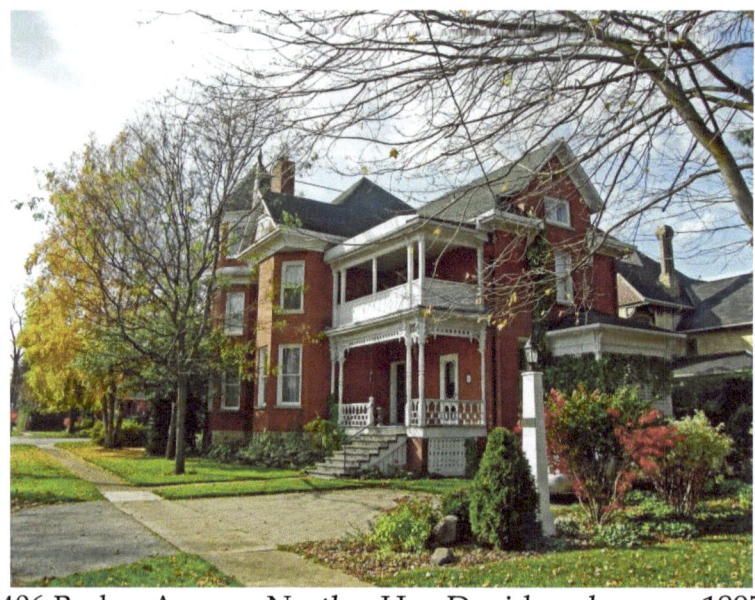

406 Barber Avenue North – Hay Davidson home c. 1895
Queen Anne Revival style

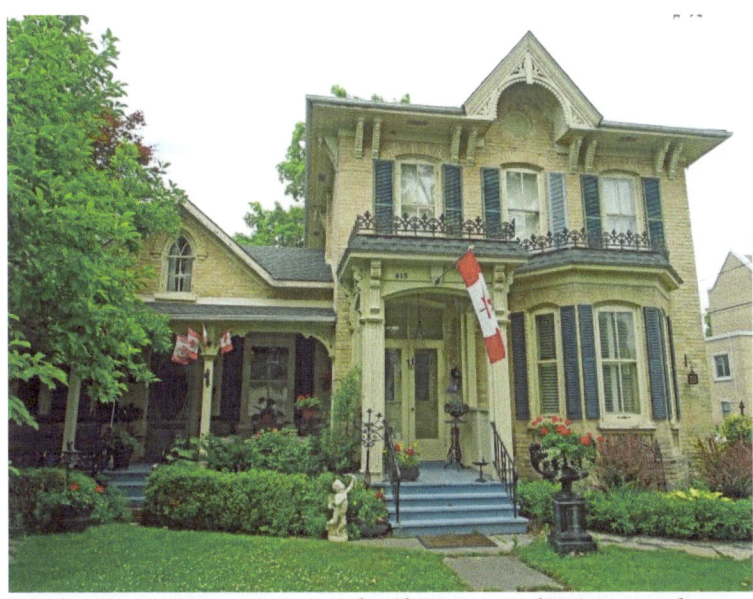

415 Inkerman Street West – built in two distinct styles – the larger east half is Italianate with paired cornice brackets, iron cresting above porch and above bay window, decorative gable; the smaller west half is rural Ontario design with a verandah

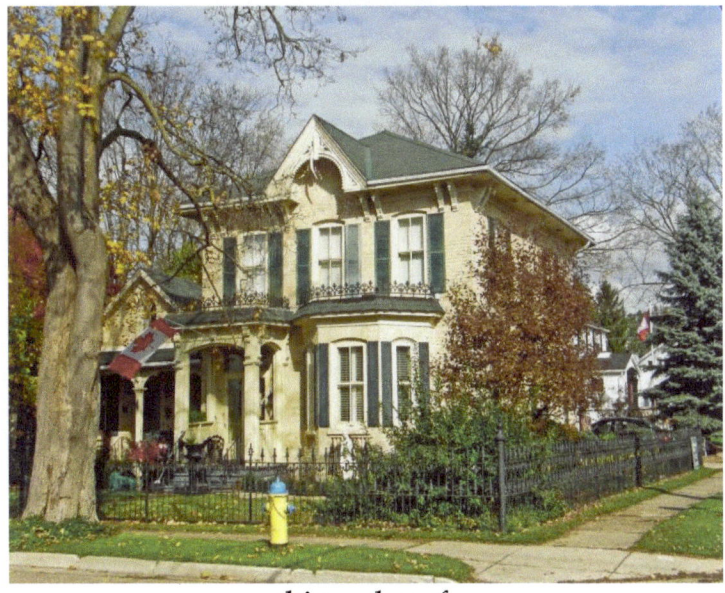

hipped roof

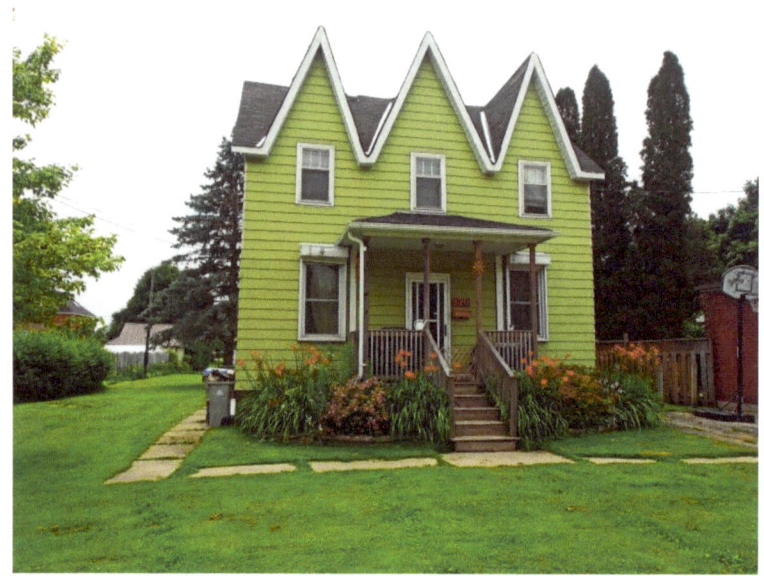

370 Inkerman Street West – triple gable Gothic Revival

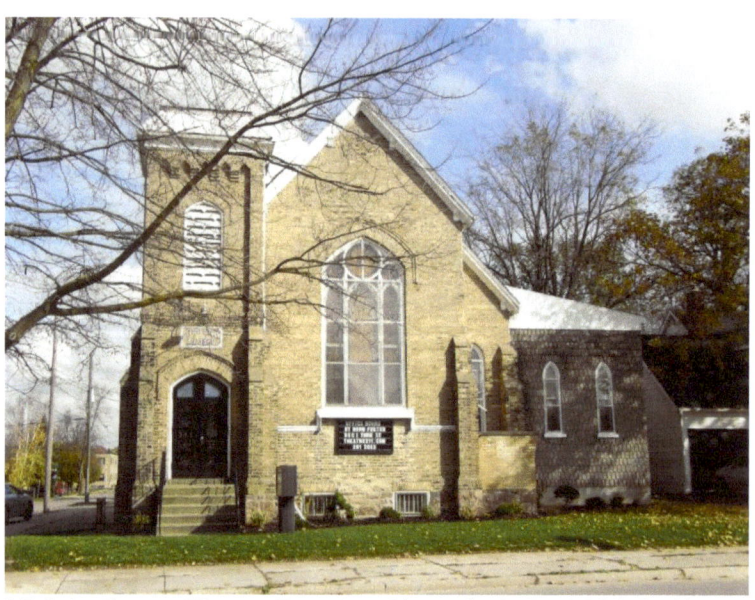

210 Main Street East – Baptist Church A.D. 1888, bell tower,
lancet windows, buttresses

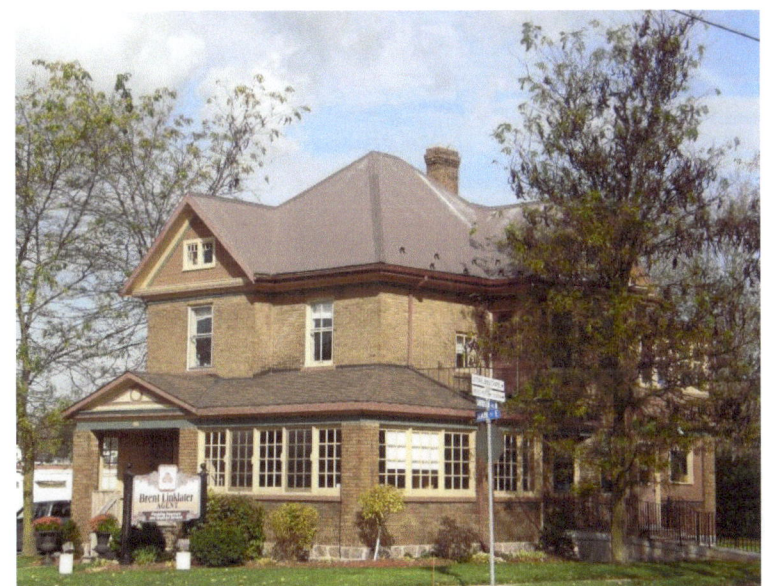

285 Main Street East

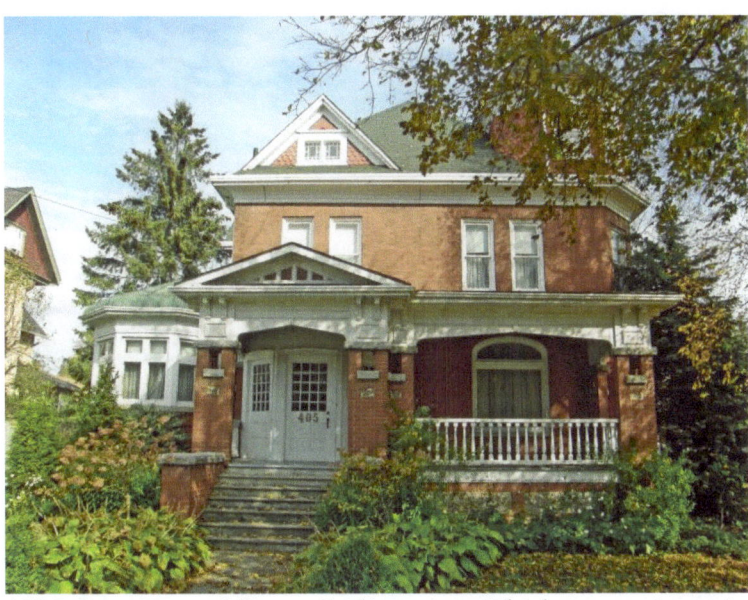

405 Main Street West – Italianate with dormers in attic,
octagonal sunroom on the side, pediment above door

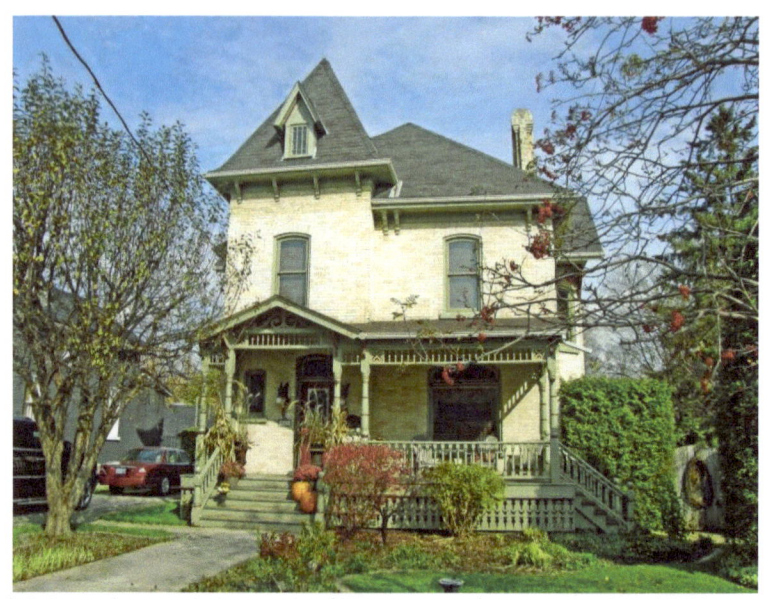

419 Main Street West – Italianate with two-and-a-half storey frontispiece with dormer

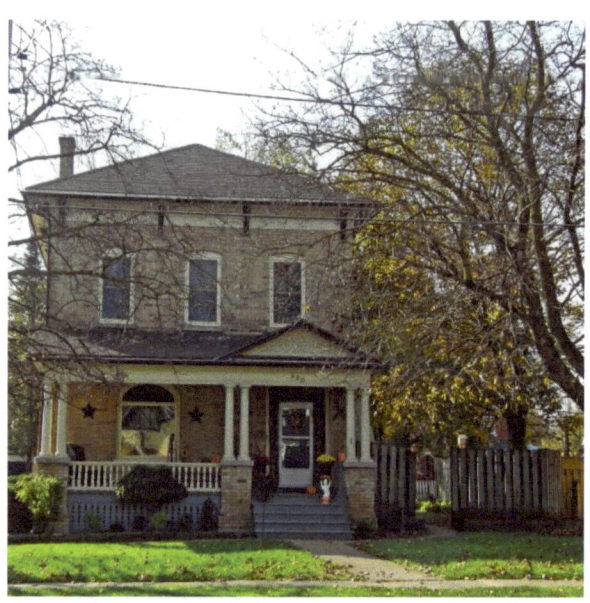

420 Main Street West – Italianate, cornice brackets, pediment, hipped roof

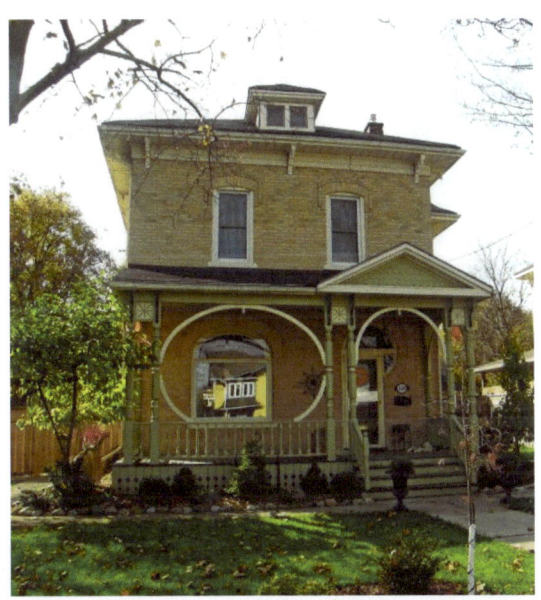

440 Main Street West – circular front verandah – Queen Anne/Italianate – original white brick was made from a marl bed near Gowanstown; pediment

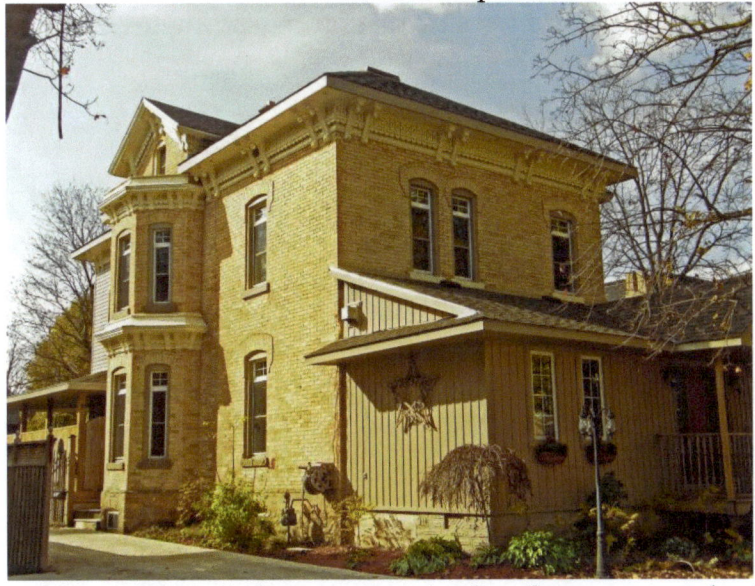

Main Street West – Italianate, cornice brackets, two-and-a-half storey tower-like bay on side of house, arched window voussoirs

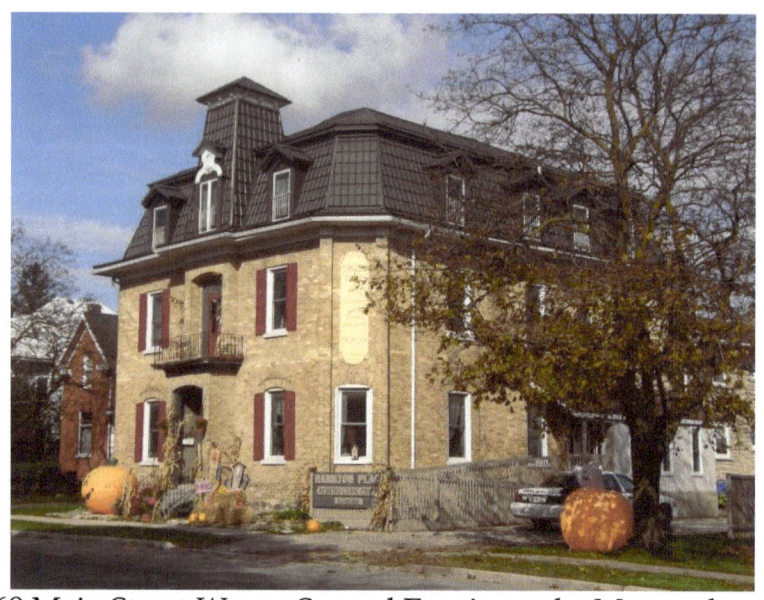

469 Main Street West – Second Empire style, Mansard roof, dormers with window hoods, built of Wallace brick – was once on edge of town and operated as the Last Chance Hotel – last chance for a drink before leaving town

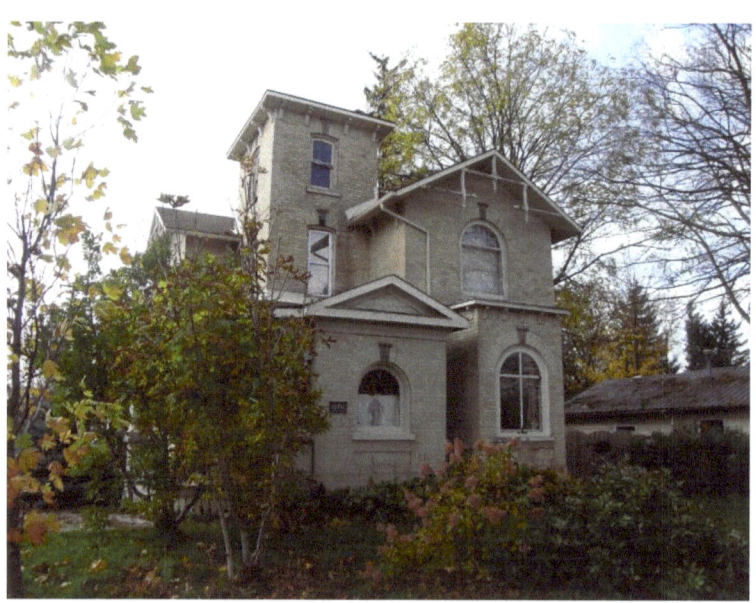

502 Main Street West – Queen Anne style

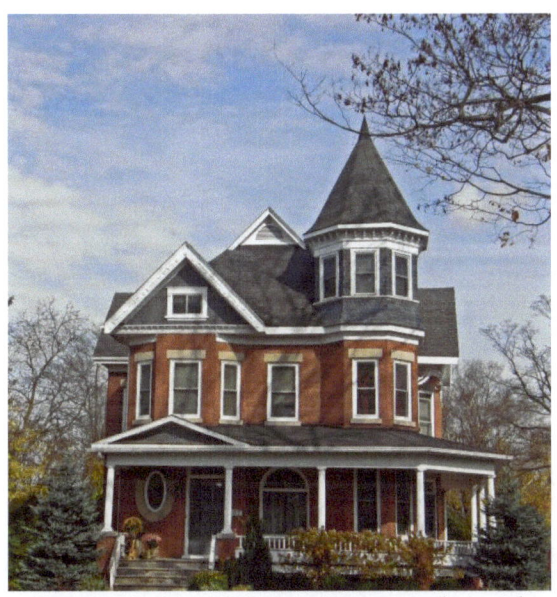

507 Main Street West – Queen Anne style with plenty of windows, chimneys and gables

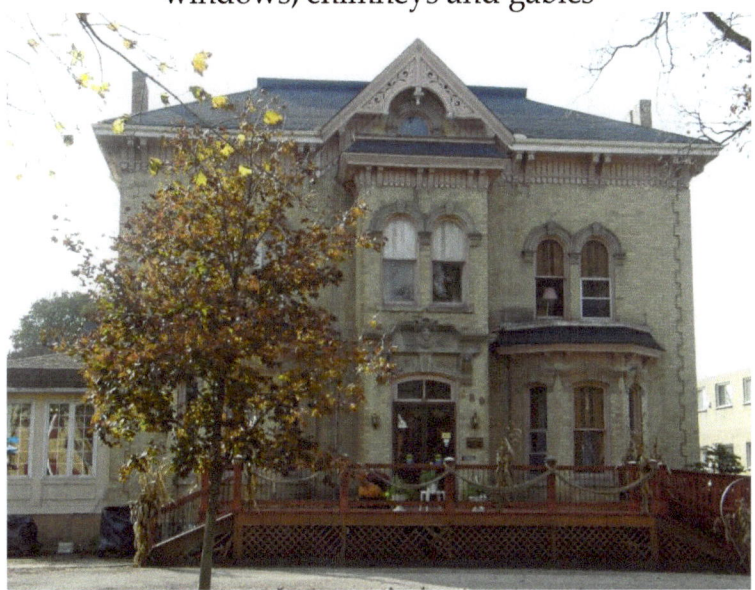

480 Main Street West – Livingstone Manor - Italianate, two-and-a-half storey tower-like bay with decorated gable, arched window voussoirs with keystones, bay window – locally produced Wallace brick, stone carvings from Scotland, marble work from Italy

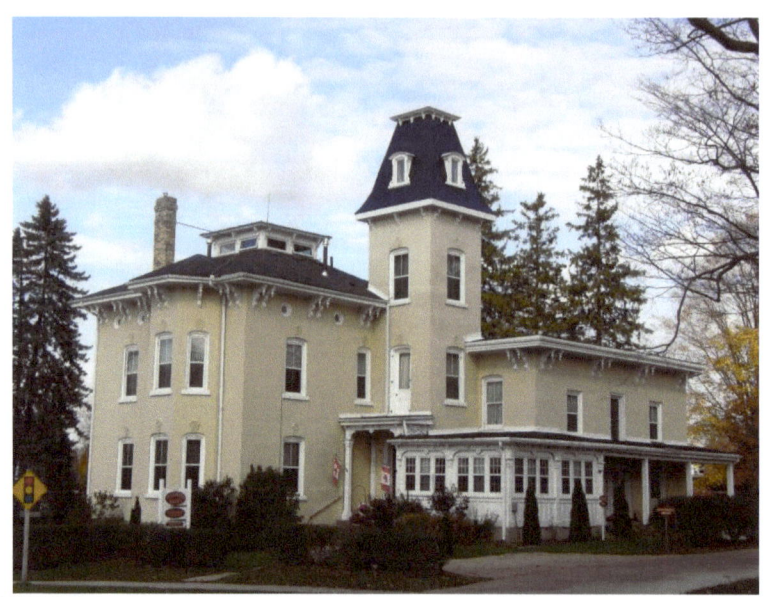

555 Main Street West – Italianate with four-storey tower, belvedere on roof – site of Listowel's first settler John Binning's log cabin; the present house is one of the oldest in town, built in 1860, tower and front half added in 1870

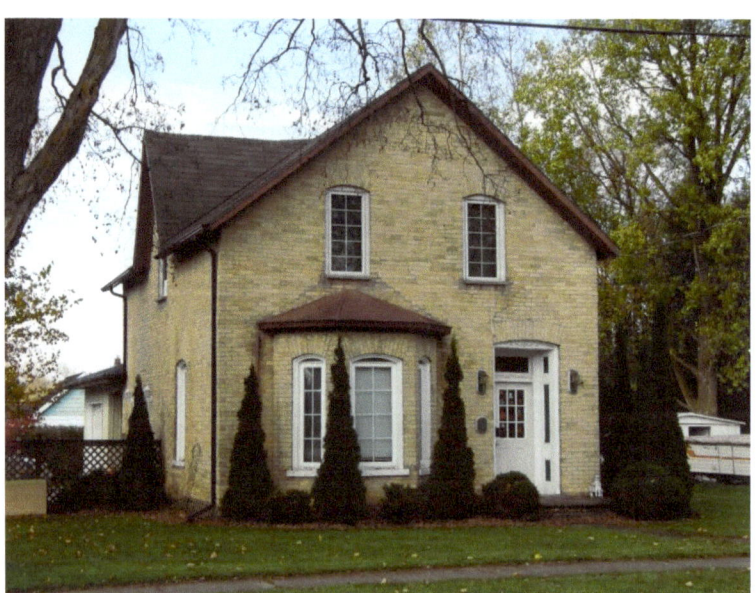

273 Main Street West – Gothic Revival

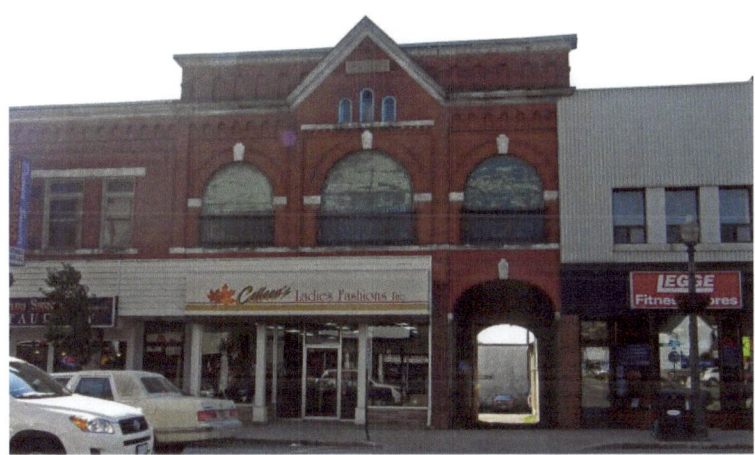

McDonald's Block – patterned brickwork, Romanesque style
arched window voussoirs with keystones

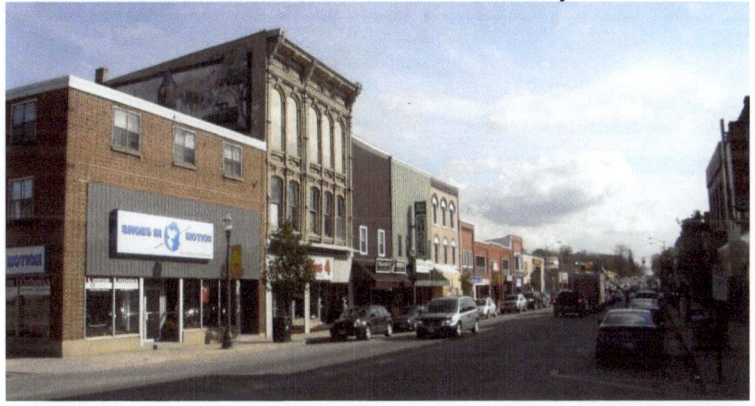

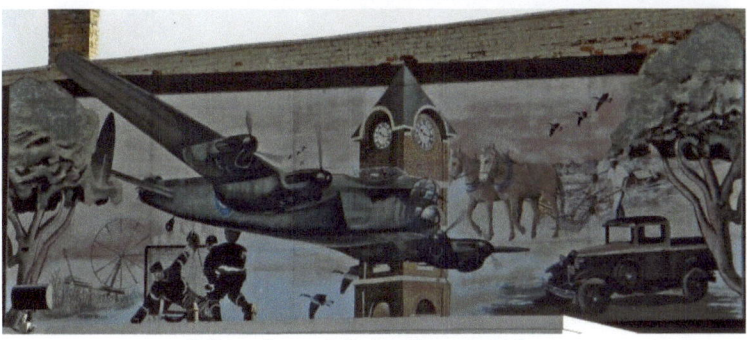

Mural on Main Street West

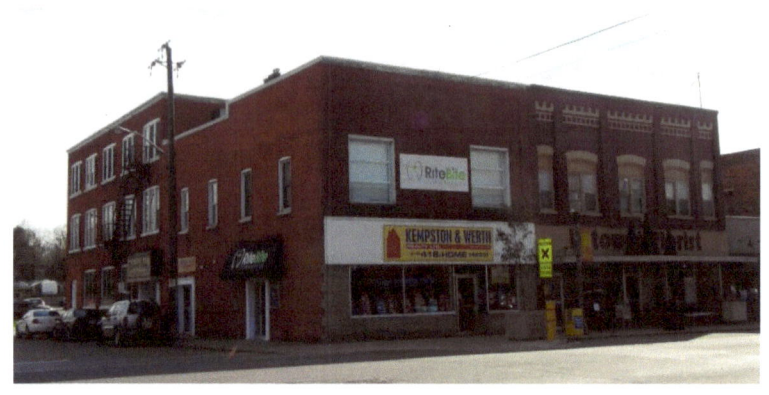

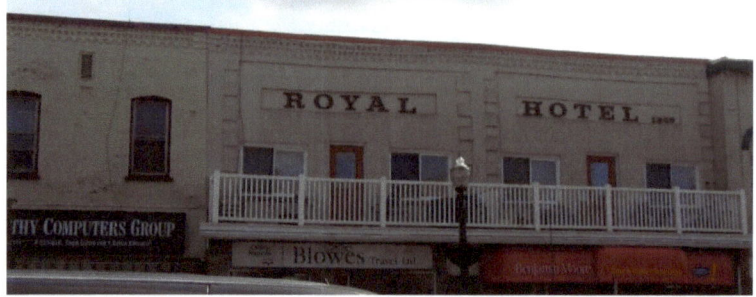

Main Street West - Royal Hotel – 1869 – dentil moulding

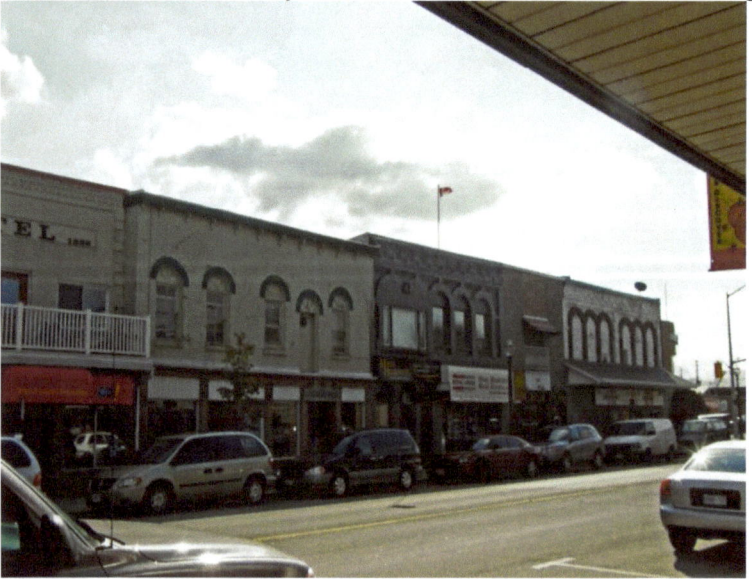

Arched window voussoirs, cornice brackets

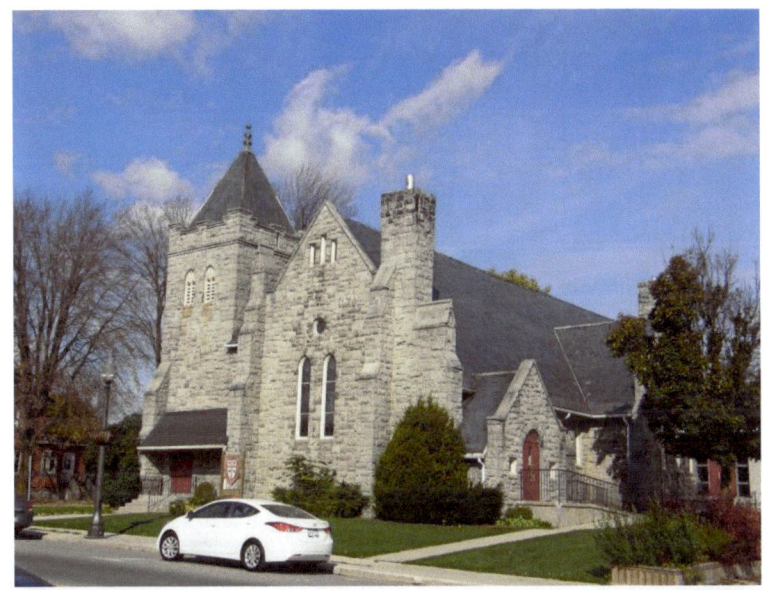

295 Main Street West – Christ Anglican Church founded 1861
Slate roof, Gothic features, narrow stained glass windows,
built in 1896

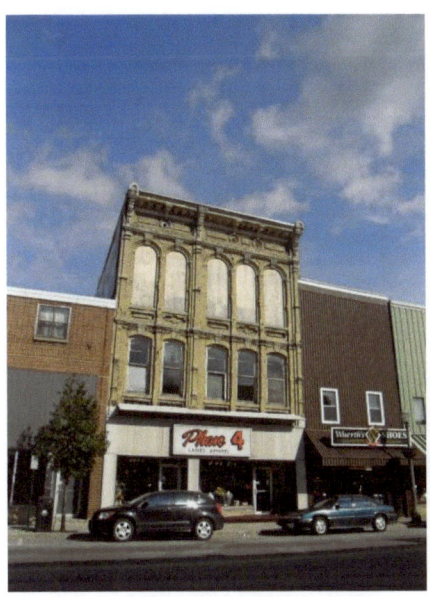

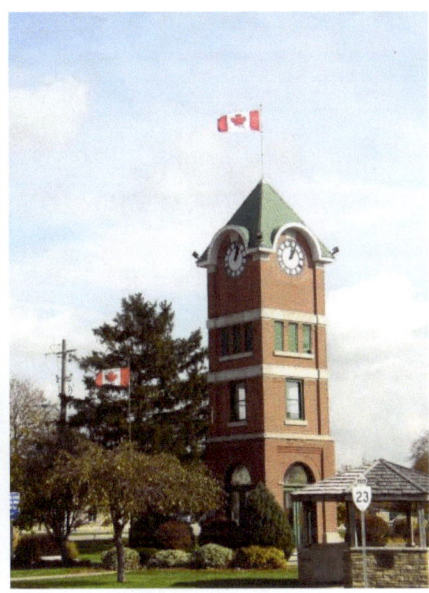

Arched window voussoirs,
Keystones, cornice brackets

Clock Tower

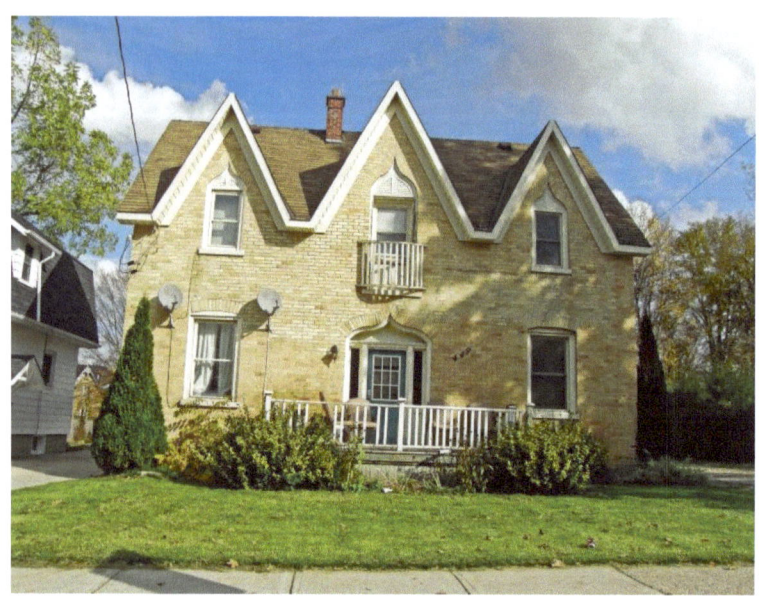

#449 – triple gable Gothic Revival,
uniquely shaped window voussoirs

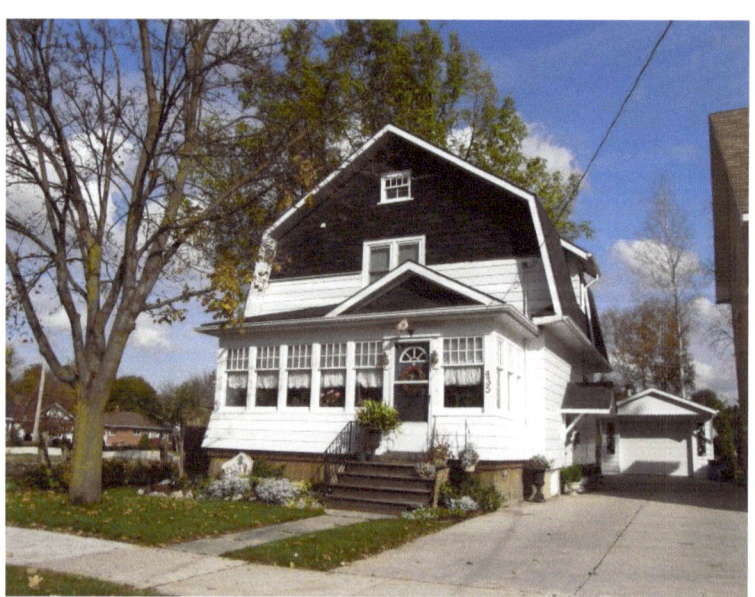

#435

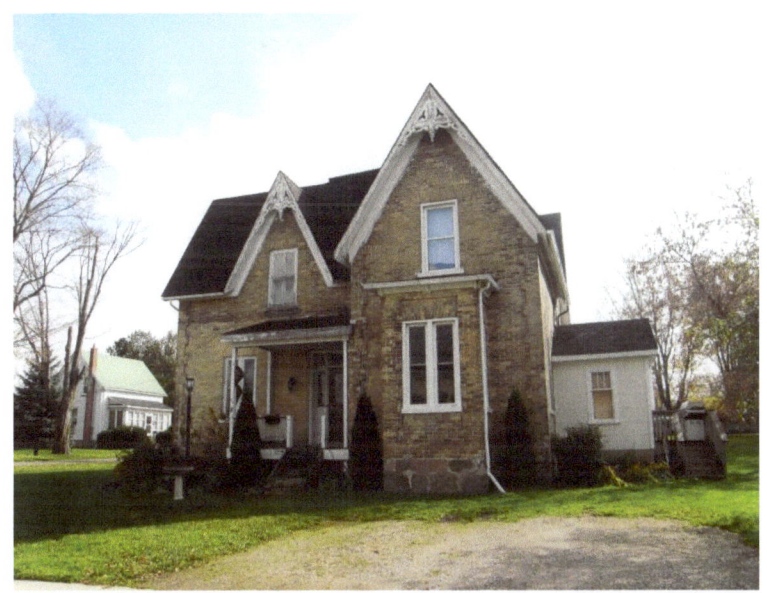

#18 – Gothic Revival, Vergeboard trim on gables, yellow brick

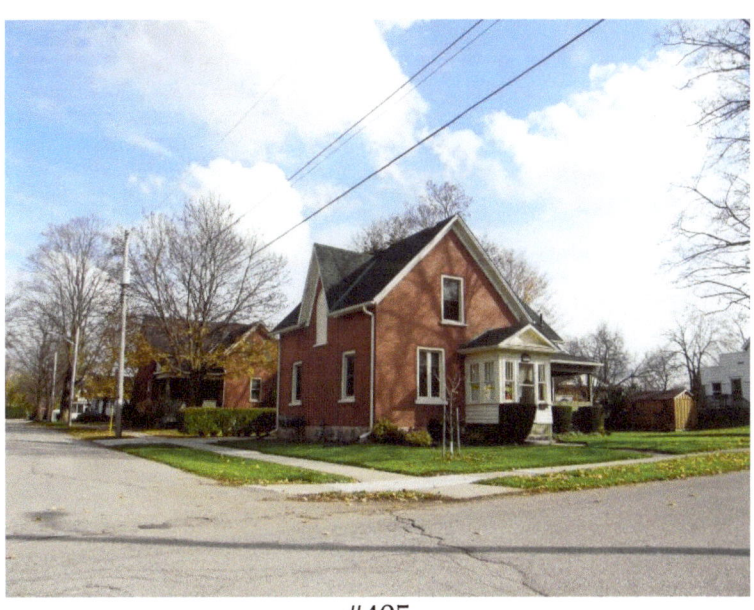

#405

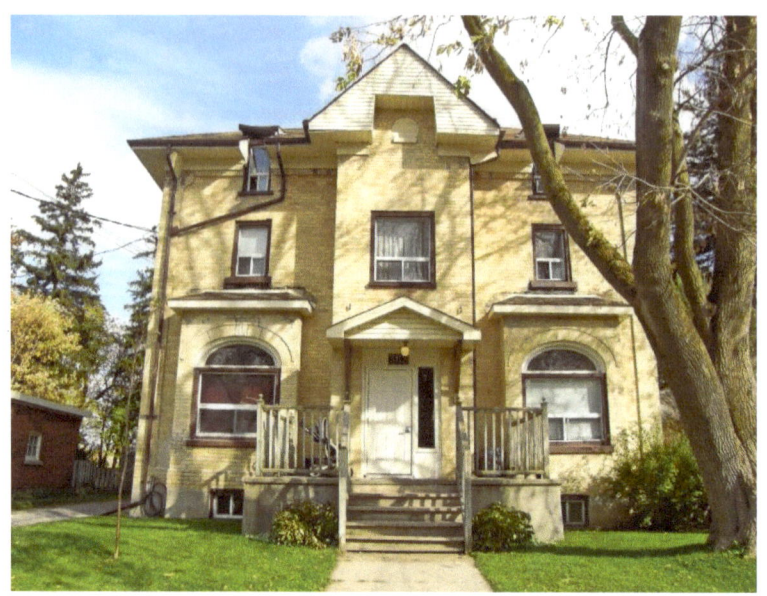

#363 – Italianate with two-storey tower-like frontispiece
topped with gable

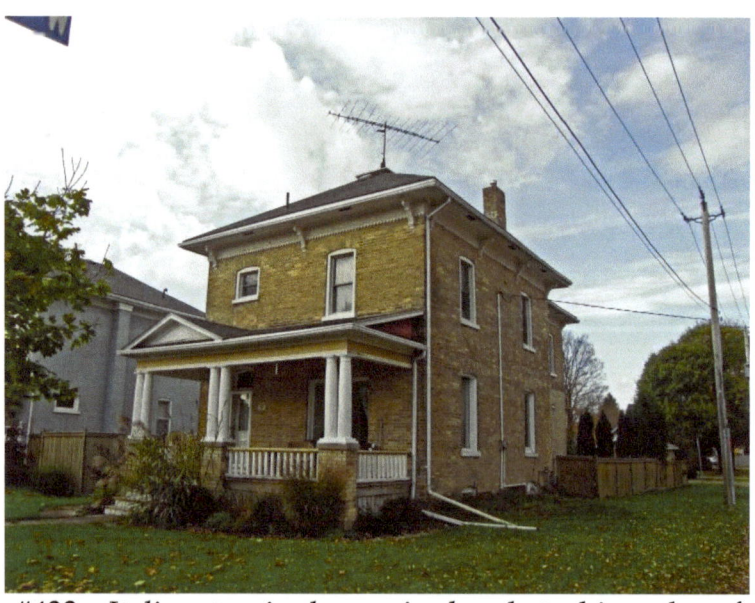

#433 – Italianate, single cornice brackets, hipped roof

Architectural Terms

Belvedere: (from the Italian "beautiful view") an architectural feature on a roof, in a garden or on a terrace that gives a beautiful view. Example: 555 Main Street West	
Brackets: a decorative or weight-bearing structural element which forms a right angle with one side against a wall and the other under a projecting surface such as an eave or roof. Example: 185 Binning Street West	
Cornice: originally the wooden overhang of the roof. With the use of stone, brick, iron and steel, the cornice is any projecting shelf at the top of a ceiling or roof. They can be very decorative. Example: 322 Binning Street West	
Cornice Return: decorative element on the end of a gable. Example: Binning Street West	
Dentil Moulding: an even series of rectangles used as ornamental decoration in cornices. Example: Main Street West, Royal Hotel	
Dormer: (French for "sleep") a gable end window that pierces through the plane of a sloping roof surface to create usable space in the top floor or attic of a building by adding headroom. Example: 230 Binning Street West	
Fretwork: interlaced decorative design resembling a bracket Example:	

Frontispiece: a portion of the façade of a building, usually a centred doorway that is slightly raised from the rest of the building, usually has extensive ornamentation. Frontispieces are usually Classical in design with white columned porches. (#363)	
Gable: the triangular portion of a wall between the edges of a sloping roof. Example: 480 Main Street West	
Hipped Roof: a roof where all sides slope downwards to the walls with no gables. Example: 525 Wallace Avenue North	
Keystones and Voussoirs: a voussoir is a wedge-shaped element used in building an arch. A keystone is the central stone that locks all the stones into position, allowing the arch to bear weight. A keystone is often enlarged and embellished. Example: 480 Main Street West	
Lancet Window: a tall, narrow window with a pointed arch at its top. Example: 150 Binning Street West, Calvary United Church	

Mansard Roof: This style was popularized by Francois Mansart (1598-1666), an accomplished architect of the French Baroque period and especially fashionable during the Second French Empire (1852-1870). This roof is almost flat on the top section, with two slopes on each of its sides with the lower slope at a steeper angle than the upper and having dormer windows. Example: 469 Main Street West	
Palladian Window: a large window that is divided into three sections with the centre section larger than the two side sections and usually arched. Example: 415 Argyle Avenue North	
Pediment: a triangular section above the horizontal structure (entablature), typically supported by columns. The inside of the triangle is called the tympanum. Example: 215 Binning Street West	
Rose Window: a circular window with ornamental tracery radiating from the centre. Example: 220 Livingstone Avenue North, Knox Presbyterian Church	
Turret: a small tower that projects from the wall of a building. Example: 220 Livingstone Avenue North, Knox Presbyterian Church	

Vergeboard and Finial: also called bargeboards – hang from the projecting end of a roof and are often elaborately carved and ornamented. **Finial:** ornament added to the top of a gable, pinnacle, canopy or spire – a Gothic element. Example: 390 Livingstone Avenue North	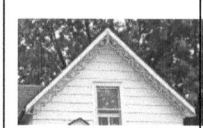
Window Hood: A **hood** is the piece found above window openings, usually of an ornate design, and covers the top third of the opening. Hoods are commonly placed above arched or curved openings on both windows and doors. Example: 469 Main Street West	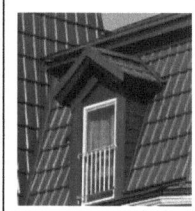

Building Styles

Edwardian, 1900-1930 – This style bridges the ornate and elaborate styles of the Victorian era and the simplified styles of the 20th century. Balanced facades, simple roof lines, dormer windows, large front porches, and smooth brick surfaces are its characteristics. Example: 445 Wallace Avenue North	
Gothic Revival, 1830-1890 – These decorative buildings have sharply-pitched gables with highly detailed vergeboards, pointed-arch window openings, and dichromatic brickwork. It is a common style in Ontario. Example: 370 Inkerman Street West	
Italianate, 1850-1900 – It has wide-bracketed eaves, belvederes, wrap-around verandahs. Example: 145 Argyle Avenue North	
Queen Anne, 1885-1900 – This style is distinguished by an irregular outline featuring a combination of an offset tower, broad gables, projecting two-storey bays, verandahs, multi-sloped roofs, and tall, decorative chimneys. A mixture of brick and wood is common. Windows often have one large single-paned bottom sash and small panes in the upper sash. Example: 507 Main Street West	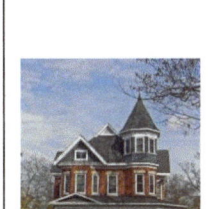

Romanesque Revival, 1880-1910 – This style hearkens back to medieval architecture of the 11th and 12th centuries with a heavy appearance, blocky towers and rounded arches. Example: 220 Livingstone Avenue North, Knox Presbyterian Church	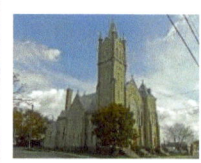
Second Empire, 1860-1880 – The mansard roof is the most noteworthy feature of this style and is evidence of the French origins. Projecting central towers and one or two-storey bays can also be present. Example: 469 Main Street West	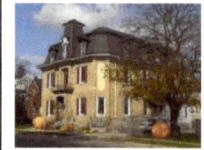

www.ingramcontent.com/pod-product-compliance
Lightning Source LLC
Chambersburg PA
CBHW040919180526
45159CB00002BA/528